BRIGHT NOTES

SHERLOCK HOLMES BY SIR ARTHUR CONAN DOYLE

Intelligent Education

Nashville, Tennessee

BRIGHT NOTES: Sherlock Holmes
www.BrightNotes.com

No part of this publication may be used or reproduced in any manner whatsoever without written permission, except in the case of brief quotations in critical articles and reviews. For permissions, contact Influence Publishers http://www.influencepublishers.com.

ISBN: 978-1-645423-98-0 (Paperback)
ISBN: 978-1-645423-99-7 (eBook)

Published in accordance with the U.S. Copyright Office Orphan Works and Mass Digitization report of the register of copyrights, June 2015.

Originally published by Monarch Press.
Mary P. De Camara; Stephen Hayes, 1977
2020 Edition published by Influence Publishers.

Interior design by Lapiz Digital Services. Cover Design by Thinkpen Designs.

Printed in the United States of America.

Library of Congress Cataloging-in-Publication Data forthcoming.
Names: Intelligent Education
Title: BRIGHT NOTES: Sherlock Holmes
Subject: STU004000 STUDY AIDS / Book Notes

CONTENTS

1)	Introduction to Sir Arthur Conan Doyle	1
2)	Introduction to Historical Background	10
3)	Abbreviations for Titles of Stories and Novels	16
4)	The Adventures of Sherlock Holmes	21
5)	The Memoirs of Sherlock Holmes	46
6)	The Return of Sherlock Holmes	67
7)	His Last Bow	93
8)	The Casebook of Sherlock Holmes	106
9)	Character Analyses	125
10)	Criticism	137

11)	Essay Questions and Answers	143
12)	Topics for Further Study	149
13)	Bibliography	151

INTRODUCTION TO SIR ARTHUR CONAN DOYLE

LIFE SPAN

Arthur Conan Doyle, eldest son of seven children of artist Charles Doyle and Mary Foley, was born at Picardy Place, Edinburgh, Scotland, on May 22, 1859. His death seventy-one years later found him world-renowned as a dedicated doctor, historical novelist, historian, sincere spiritualist, and creator of the world's most famous detective.

EDUCATION

Doyle received his early education at Stonyhurst College in Lancashire. After studying an additional year at the Jesuit Feldkirch in Austria, he surprised his artistic family by choosing medicine as his career. He received his medical degrees in 1881 and 1885 at the Edinburgh University where he had two professors who would later serve as models for his literary characters.

INSTRUCTORS

In his autobiographical *Memories and Adventures* (1924), Doyle describes Professor Rutherford with his "Assyrian beard, his prodigious voice, his enormous chest and his singular manner" and readers recognize these traits in Professor Challenger, a character in Doyle's science-fiction novels - *The Lost World* (1912); *The Poison Belt* (1913); and *The Land of Mist* (1926). Doyle traced his love for science fiction back to his boyhood days when he had read Jules Verne in French.

More far-reaching was his association with Dr. Joseph Bell whose deductive method of reasoning began with the patient's entrance into the waiting room where the surgeon observed him carefully. Before the diagnosis was pronounced, Dr. Bell had often inferred the occupation of the person and much about his character.

PRACTICE

To meet expenses, Dr. Doyle signed up as a naval surgeon and took two voyages, which would furnish him with material for further writing: *The Stark Munro Letters*, which has many autobiographical features, and *The Captain of the Polestar*.

Dr. Doyle set up his practice as oculist in Southsea, Portsmouth, England. Patients were few and far between, and he used his waiting hours to write. In 1885 he married Louise Hawkins, "Touie," the daughter of one of his patients. It was now imperative to write.

INFLUENCES

Doyle attributed his love for letters and his instinct for storytelling to his mother, "Ma'am," who traced her ancestry back to Sir Walter Scott. Love for all that was heroic and medieval stemmed from his mother and found expression in his historical novels at a later date.

One of his boyhood heroes was Auguste Dupin, the masterful detective of Edgar Allan Poe, Father of the Detective Story. To Poe he was indebted for the idea of an eccentric detective who used observation, logic, and deduction to solve his cases. Dupin had his admiringly obtuse friend to chronicle his cases and serve as a foil. Doyle was also attracted to the figure Lecoq, detective created by Emile Gaboriau whose dovetailing plots so intrigued him.

Finally, Doyle conceived the idea of creating his own detective after the manner of Dr. Joseph Bell with his "eerie trick of spotting details." Doyle reasoned that if this deductive method was so successful in real life, he could certainly make it plausible in fiction. He said that he "tried to build up a man who pushed the thing as far as it would go - further, occasionally."

NAMES

Originally, Doyle planned to call his sleuth "Sherrinford Holmes." The surname was a tribute to a man he greatly admired in America, Oliver Wendell Holmes, senior. The first name was that of a cricketer with whom he had played. His detective would not have an anonymous partner as did Dupin; the narrator would be called Ormond Sacker. The first novel to feature the pair would be entitled "A Tangled Skein". Before publication, happy changes occurred: Sherrinford became Sherlock; Ormond Sacker was changed to John H. Watson (after an army friend, Colonel James Watson); and the novel was published by Ward, Lock and Company in 1887 as *A Study in Scarlet*, bringing the author twenty-five pounds. *The Lippincott Magazine* in America commissioned him for a second novel and he produced *The Sign of Four* in 1890.

SERIES

In 1891 the *Strand Magazine* started the celebrated series of twelve short stories, each complete in itself, that would later be published (1892) as *The Adventures of Sherlock Holmes*. It was dedicated to Dr. Joseph Bell.

HISTORICAL NOVELS

As early as 1888, Doyle had tried his hand at writing historical novels. *Micah Clark* dealt with the Monmouth Rebellion. This was followed by shorter novels on the Napoleonic Wars. *The White Company* (1890), *The Refugees* (1893), *Rodney Stone* (1896), and *Sir Nigel* (1906) have all been eclipsed by what the author considered inferior writing, the detective stories (most of which he wrote within a week). To them, Doyle owes his literary immortality; at the time, however, he felt their popularity detracted from his more serious endeavors. After publishing the second series of stories, *The Memoirs of Sherlock Holmes*, he was determined never to write about sleuths again.

MORATORIUM

What the most treacherous enemies of Holmes failed to accomplish - get the sleuth off the scene - his creator attempted. But he too failed. He had insinuated in the last story, "The Final Problem," that Holmes, locked in mortal combat with the Napoleon of Crime, Professor Moriarty, had fallen over the famous Reichenbach Falls along with the villain. Holmes had vouched earlier that he would consider it a supreme triumph to rid the world of such an evil force and that death itself would not be too high a price to pay.

RESURRECTION

Protesters went so far as to wear arm bands in mourning for their favorite sleuth. For nine years, though, Doyle held firm. Public clamoring, a deluge of protest mail, formation of "Keep Holmes Alive" societies, all exerted a pressure that Doyle might have found difficult to resist indefinitely. The public would not allow the myth to die. In the end, what prompted Doyle to begin writing detective stories caused him to return to them: he needed funds. He had a growing interest in spiritualism and, in order to preach its gospel, he had to have funds. Thus, he resurrected Holmes. He did not commit himself to more than a single novel which he termed "pre-Reichenbach." In 1902 he dated *The Hound of the Baskervilles* prior to "The Final Problem."

But fans hounded him and expenses forced him to resurrect Holmes. Doyle used the supposition that Holmes had gone underground for three years to unravel the complicated web of iniquity spun by the late Moriarty. Three volumes of short stories and, one novel followed: *The Return of Sherlock Holmes* (1905); the novel, *The Valley of Fear* (1915); *His Last Bow* (1917); and *The Casebook* (1927). Critics tend to agree with the fan who told Doyle that Holmes was never quite the same after his Reichenbach experience. The earlier stories are considered to be superior.

The sixty adventures (fifty-six short stories and four novels) are referred to as the saga or Canon. (Stories not considered to be Doyle's are termed apocryphal.)

KNIGHTHOOD

Doyle was actively engaged in the Boer War (1889-1902) offering medical assistance at the Langman Field Hospital in Bloemfontein and writing the history of the war (1900) plus a pamphlet vindicating the British Army. In 1902 his services were acknowledged with knighthood. He wanted to decline the honor but his mother, to whom he was so devoted, feared he might insult the new king, Edward VII, by refusing. (Doyle saw to it that Holmes was offered the very same honor in the exact year in "The Three Garridebs" and Holmes would not accept it.)

CRIMINOLOGIST

In real life, Doyle was consulted like his famous detective, and in two cases women begged him to locate their missing fiances as he had Holmes do in several stories. He succeeded in locating one, but persuaded the woman that she was fortunate he had disappeared.

Doyle took a great interest in public affairs and either joined or spearheaded causes where he felt justice had been denied. Along with prominent persons like George Bernard Shaw, Beatrice and Sidney Webb, G. K. Chesterton, he worked to have the death penalty lifted from Roger Casement, a traitor during World War I, on grounds that the man was not responsible. Doyle was not successful.

With Oscar Slater, however, Doyle established a reputation as a criminologist and champion of the oppressed. Sentenced to death, Slater had a reprieve and had served eighteen years of a life term when Doyle took up his case. He brought it to public notice by writing and succeeded in stirring up a controversy.

Slater was released and wrote to Doyle: "Sir Conan Doyle, I thank you from the bottom of my heart for the goodness you have shown towards me." By a special act of Parliament, Doyle succeeded in having a retrial.

Doyle helped pave the way for the Court of Criminal Appeal in England. Thanks to his untiring efforts, George Edalji was released after serving three years of a seven-year sentence in a case that sounds like an English version of the French Dreyfus affair. Great as his record was, however, Doyle failed to win a seat in Parliament after two attempts.

SPIRITUALISM

His wife Touie died in 1906 and he remarried a year later. He had two children by his first wife (Mary and Kingsley) and three by his second, Jean Leckie (Denis, Adrian, and Jean). His son Kingsley died of pneumonia after being badly wounded at the Somme. The son's death only intensified Doyle's already strong interest in spiritualism. In 1921 he wrote *The Wonderings of a Spiritualist*, and in 1926, *History of Spiritualism*. He and his wife lectured across the country and in America. In his own words, "All other work which I have ever done, or could ever do, was as nothing compared with this."

DEATH

Doyle spent the early months of 1930 on a lecture tour of the Continent. When he returned he was physically exhausted and suffered from angina pectoris. Conscious of his critical condition, he said, "I am quite prepared to go or stay, for I know that life and love, go on forever." His earthly life terminated on

July 7, 1930, at 9:30 a.m., at his home in Crowborough, Sussex. He was buried in the Minstead churchyard, New Forest, one of his favorite places, often mentioned in his writings. His epitaph reads:

> **Steel true**
> **Blade straight**
> **Arthur Conan Doyle**
> **Knight**
> **Patriot, Physician, and Man of Letters**

ESTATE

The Doyle literary estate is one of the richest in the world. His son, Adrian M. Conan Doyle, established the eleventh-century Chateau de Lucens in Switzerland as a fitting memorial, replete with Doyle's papers, letters, and biographical memorabilia. It houses the third and finest of the "Sherlock Holmes Rooms," a replica of the famous 221B Baker Street.

PUBLICATIONS

In England there is *The Sherlock Holmes Journal* published biannually; America has a quarterly, *The Baker Street Journal*. Holmes was the first fictional character to have a full-length biography written about him. In addition, there are encyclopedias, commentaries, an atlas, almanac, concordance, and glossary. The Canon has been published in over forty languages, and Holmes can be found in every genre including the musical and the ballet.

MOVIES

Holmes was the subject of silent films as early as 1903. The first actor to take the part was the Danish Forrest Holger-Madsen; the most popular actor in the role seems to have been Basil Rathbone with Nigel Bruce starring as Watson. There have been at least seventeen versions of The Hound of the Baskervilles. While over a hundred films have been produced, many use only the character of Holmes with an original story. What better proof is there of his enduring popularity than the fact that authors and directors of each generation want to try their hand at lighting the Master's calabash!

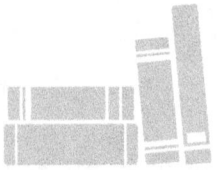

INTRODUCTION TO HISTORICAL BACKGROUND

Of Holmes, William Bolitho said: "He is more than a man; he is the spirit of a town and a time." Indeed, one finds in the Sherlock Holmes stories one of the most vivid pictures of Victorian England, especially London, to be found outside of Dickens. (While Dickens dwelt mainly in the lower class and Doyle preferred the bourgeoisie, both authors overlapped and provided a fairly broad view of the social spectrum.) Part of Holmes' charm is surely the gaslit, romantic London in which he plied his trade; and while one may learn a good deal about the times from the stories themselves, it may be helpful to have a brief historical background.

THE MONARCH

The age was called Victorian, and the name has never been questioned. It is unmistakably the period of Queen Victoria (1819-1901), who dominated England as ruler for 64 of her 82 years. Unpopular during the early part of Holmes' career (which began after his graduation from the University, around 1876-77) because of her prolonged mourning for her dead consort Albert which seemed to obliterate the nation's interests in her mind, she gradually returned to public life. In the last two decades of her reign, which included her golden and diamond jubilees (1887 and 1897), she became extremely popular among all classes. The industrial revolution, the rise of the middle class, and the successful execution of a series of wars aimed at increasing British influence made the England of the late 1880's a uniquely complacent nation - often at the expense of the lower class, whose needs and cries for social reform went unheeded in a wave of middle-class smugness.

PRIME MINISTERS

Of the several ministers who served during the Holmes Victorian era, only Benjamin Disraeli truly gained the queen's confidence with his intensely imperialist policies and by allowing her a free hand in much of the country's policy. William Gladstone, although brilliant, was too intellectual for Victoria's taste; he also proved more interested in social reform. Gascoyne-Cecil, Marquis of Salisbury, was more popular than Gladstone because he promoted a Disraeliesque policy of expansion and British superiority.

WARS

Domestic England seemed untouched by external influence, but the country was actively involved in many empire-expanding wars during the period of Holmes' practice: the Indian Wars which secured Victoria the added title "Empress of India"; the Crimean War, in process when Holmes was born (1854), to prevent Russian expansion; the Afghan campaign in which Watson was wounded. Fighting began in 1878 when the leader of Afghanistan denied entrance to British envoys while opening Afghanistan to Russians. This prompted Disraeli to send British troops to counter the hostility. It was in the "fatal battle of Maiwand," July 1880, that Watson received the wound which sent him back to England; Disraeli was also "wounded" in this war. The large number of British casualties shocked the general public and this, along with his poor handling of domestic economy, led to his subsequent defeat by Gladstone.

LAWS AND SOCIAL REFORM

The class structure of England was as strict as - if not stricter than - it had always been; yet this very fact gave rise to the beginnings of social upheaval and struggles for reform. Labor gained a voice in government with the 1884 Voting Reform Bill, providing for universal male suffrage. Although the struggle for women's rights did not appear until Edward's reign, women were beginning to break free of the traditional "dependent" role. This change in social attitudes is reflected in Holmes' female clients who make independent livings as typists, governesses, etc. Two social reform topics which caused much debate during Holmes' era were drugs and divorce: the Drug Act had not yet been passed in England, and it was acceptable for people of all classes to indulge in a "seven-percent solution" - as Holmes often did - in the comfort of their own homes, or in a pipeful of opium in the sordid dens of the East End (See MANW*). This leniency is in contrast with the traditional strictness of anti-divorce laws, which Doyle fought so vehemently (DEVI, ABBE). The unsafe, unhealthy living conditions of the poor as compared to the luxury of the upper classes were only beginning to come to light, thanks to the efforts of such writers as Dickens, Wilde, and the young George Bernard Shaw, and such dramatic events as the Ripper slayings of 1888.

SCOTLAND YARD

As the laws of England changed, so did the law enforcement agencies. Sir Robert Peel, English Home Secretary (after whom "bobbies" and "peelers" are named) was responsible for the founding of the first Scotland Yard in 1829 which was also the first organized police force in the world. Backing Scotland Yard Line, the first building was the headquarters of the London Metropolitan Police. Not until 40 years later did the first plain-clothes detectives appear, and gradually the term "Scotland Yard" came to refer only to the Criminal Investigations Department. In 1890 Scotland Yard moved to a new building (now called "Old Scotland Yard") on the Thames. Early criminal arrests depended solely on personal description and witnesses (who were more often than not undercover agents - a popular device of the Yard during the Holmesian era). Not until 1895 did English scientist Sir William Herschel discover that fingerprints were unique, providing the first practical and infallible system of identification. Another traditional Scotland Yard institution was that of policemen without guns.

MONEY

The currency of the Holmes stories may present some difficulty to the reader unfamiliar with English coinage before their change to decimalization in 1969. A pound consisted of 20 shillings; a shilling was 12 pence and, therefore, there were 240 pence in a pound. The halfpenny (hay'penny), three-pence (thruppence), sixpence (tanner), quarter-penny (farthing) were figured accordingly. A florin was two shillings; a guinea was one pound, one shilling (or 21 shillings). The symbol for pound was (L), shillings were denoted by the letter "s." and pence by "d." Prices figured in shillings and pence were often written thus:

15/6, i.e., 15 shillings and sixpence. In Holmes' time the pound was equal to approximately 5 American dollars; a shilling, 25 cents. The resulting value of various items in the Canon may be approximated from this.

TRANSPORTATION AND COMMUNICATION

The Holmes medium of communication par excellence was the telegraph, which necessitated the terse, concise wording which appealed to Holmes' logical mind. It was incredibly quick, delivered to the Central Post Office via pneumatic tubes and dispatched with the utmost haste. It was inexpensive, sixpence for twelve words, and readily accessible from many branch stations. The mail service itself was quick and frequent: often five or more daily deliveries in the larger cities. Many of Holmes' communiques bear the time of day, rather than the date, atop the letter. Also highly efficient, and highly in evidence in the Holmes stories, was the train service (both above and underground) which was convenient to Holmes at the nearby Baker Street station of the Metropolitan Railway. Between stations ran other modes of conveyance - horse-drawn buses and a multitude of cabs and carriages for the more fashionable: broughams, two-wheelers, hansoms, baroques.

LONDON

Holmes' city was, and still is, divided into unique sections. The West End was the section of the rich, the ruling class and government, the clubbers, theatergoers, and shoppers. One finds here a plethora of residential areas (including Baker Street); huge, lovely Hyde Park and Kensington Gardens where the upper classes took their strolls and Sunday afternoon amusements; fashionable shops (Oxford Street, Bond Street, Regent Street, Picadilly Circus); government buildings (along Whitehall and the Victoria Embankment are found the Houses of Parliament, No. 10 Downing Street, and Mycroft's beloved Admiralty Offices); theaters and popular, bawdy music-houses of the day as well as London's famous "clubland" (playground of the wealthy, snobbish and misanthropic, of which the Diogenes Club was a part); St. James' Street, Haymarket, Pall Mall, and up the Strand to Aldwych. Moving east through legal London (the Temple and Royal Courts, along the Embankment and Carey Street) and pressland - Fleet Street, home of London's newspapers - takes one to the East End. This was the section of the poor: the sailors, laborers, streetwalkers and opium addicts. Beginning within the square-mile section which was the original London and is now known as "the City," and heading east from St. Paul's, lay the street markets, the churches, the opium dens, and portside taverns. Ironically, part of this squalid London that Holmes knew well is sandwiched between the Tower of London, symbol of English royalty and wealth since William the Conqueror, and the financial London of Threadneedle Street.

This, then, was Holmes' London truly, as Watson says in STUD, "that great cesspool into which all the loungers and idlers of the Empire are irresistibly drained" - the criminals as well and, on their heels, Holmes, the champion of justice. To know him is also to know his city and his age.

* Abbreviations used in critical discussion of the Holmes stories are explained in the next section.

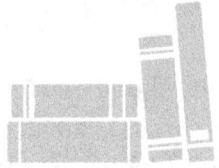

ABBREVIATIONS FOR TITLES OF STORIES AND NOVELS

The abbreviations adopted by *The Baker Street Journal* (the first four letters of the title) will be used throughout this book.

THE ADVENTURES OF SHERLOCK HOLMES

1. A Scandal in Bohemia (SCAN)
2. The Red-Headed League (REDH)
3. A Case of Identity (CASE)
4. The Boscombe Valley Mystery (BOSC)
5. The Five Orange Pips (FIVE)
6. The Man with the Twisted Lip (MANW)
7. The Blue Carbuncle (BLUE)
8. The Speckled Band (SPEC)

9. The Engineer's Thumb (ENGI)

10. The Noble Bachelor (NOBL)

11. The Beryl Coronet (BERY)

12. The Copper Beeches (COPP)

THE MEMOIRS OF SHERLOCK HOLMES

13. Silver Blaze (SILV)

14. The Yellow Face (YELL)

15. The Stockbroker's Clerk (STOC)

16. The Musgrave Ritual (MUSG)

17. The "Gloria Scott" (GLOR)

18. The Reigate Puzzle (REIG)

19. The Crooked Man (CROO)

20. The Resident Patient (RESI)

21. The Greek Interpreter (GREE)

22. The Naval Treaty (NAVA)

23. The Final Problem (FINA)

THE RETURN OF SHERLOCK HOLMES

24. The Empty House (EMPT)

25. The Norwood Builder (NORW)

26. The Dancing Men (DANC)

27. The Solitary Cyclist (SOLI)

28. The Priory School (PRIO)

29. Black Peter (BLAC)

30. Charles Augustus Milverton (CHAR)

31. The Six Napoleons (SIXN)

32. The Three Students (3STU)

33. The Golden Pince-nez (GOLD)

34. The Missing Three Quarter (MISS)

35. The Abbey Grange (ABBE)

36. The Second Stain (SECO)

HIS LAST BOW

37. Wisteria Lodge (WIST)

38. The Cardboard Box (CARD)

39. The Red Circle (REDC)

40. The Bruce-Partington Plans (BRUC)

41. The Dying Detective (DYIN)

42. The Disappearance of Lady Frances Carfax (DISA)

43. The Devil's Foot (DEVI)

44. His Last Bow (HISL)

THE CASEBOOK OF SHERLOCK HOLMES

45. The Illustrious Client (ILLU)

46. The Blanched Soldier (BLAN)

47. The Mazarin Stone (MAZA)

48. The Three Gables (3GAB)

49. The Sussex Vampire (SUSS)

50. The Three Garridebs (3GAR)

51. Thor Bridge (THOR)

52. The Creeping Man (CREE)

53. The Lion's Mane (LION)

54. The Veiled Lodger (VEIL)

55. Shoscombe Old Place (SHOS)

56. The Retired Colourman (RETI)

THE NOVELS

57. A Study in Scarlet (STUD)

58. The Sign of Four (SIGN)

59. The Hound of The Baskervilles (HOUN)

60. The Valley of Fear (VALL)

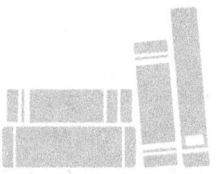

THE ADVENTURES OF SHERLOCK HOLMES

"A SCANDAL IN BOHEMIA"

This first of twelve stories in the series *The Adventures of Sherlock Holmes* is worthy of its position. As prototype, it gives a profile of Holmes and establishes a pattern that will appear in story after story. Most adventures open at 221B Baker Street with a dialogue between Holmes and Watson which is sometimes the most intriguing part of the story. Holmes usually informs his partner of a recent communique and, within moments, the client in question arrives. The worried visitor is duly impressed by what Holmes reveals about him from observations made within minutes. Confident that he is in the presence of an extraordinary detective, the guest describes his plight.

Disguise: With the exception of Watson, all of the principal characters try their hand at disguise (Holmes, twice). The royal client is the least successful and discards his mask as soon as Holmes addresses him as "Your Majesty." Holmes recognized the King of Bohemia before he even spoke, so his voice was not the revealing factor. Most likely, his extraordinary height, his exclusive stationery, and his desire to remain incognito were all the sleuth needed to deduce his identity.

A master at disguise, Holmes impersonates a drunken groom and an injured clergyman. His worthy adversary (Irene Adler) has the spunk to bid him good night in male attire. Never again in the pages of the saga will a battle of wits end so happily for everyone involved, with the participants forming a mutual admiration society.

Drugs: Watson explains but does not excuse his friend's use of cocaine (the seven-percent solution!). Occasionally, Holmes will tease his doctor companion about his efforts to wean him from this vice. For last mention of the drug, see MISS. (In England, the Drug Act was not passed until 1923.)

Watson: From the lips of the Master, one of the roles of Watson is defined: "I am lost without my Boswell." (James Boswell wrote the first modern biography, in the eighteenth century, recording the deeds and conversations of Samuel Johnson.) Watson the narrator claims to be recording this case to explain why Irene Adler will always be The woman in the mind of Holmes.

Character Study: Doyle apparently wanted to exclude from the outset any possibility of love affairs in the life of the perfectly rational Holmes. This story does not qualify as a tale of real detection, but it is probably the greatest character study of Holmes in the Canon. Characteristics that will reveal themselves in full later are his impatience with pomposity (see NOBL); dry sense of humor; cold, precise nature, need for mental or chemical stimulation; admiration for the talents of an opponent.

The King: This character is greatly overdrawn, so much the easier for Holmes to deflate. Conjectures about his true identity include Franz Ferdinand, the heir presumptive; the Grand Duke Rudolph, Prince of Bohemia; Crown Prince Wilhelm von Hohenzollern of Prussia; and even, in the opinion of Edgar Smith, Edward, Prince of Wales.

Irony: Irony (a result, the reverse of what was expected) abounds in this story. The cold intellectual is the only person wanting a souvenir of the case (photo of Irene); the beautiful woman with a resolutely "masculine" mind outwits King and Detective; the brilliant Holmes unwittingly serves as a witness (the sole one mentioned) to the marriage of The woman in his life; and the detective is the most willing to break the law.

Debt To Poe: Although Doyle will have Holmes refer to Poe's detective Dupin as an "inferior fellow," he was not above using some of Dupin's tricks: compare the eccentricities and habits of Dupin, including smoking a meerschaum pipe, to those of Holmes; recall Dupin's admiring companion-narrator and the slow police force against which Dupin's brilliance was contrasted. This comparison is especially clear in SCAN where the ruse Holmes uses to gain the photograph, and the whole basis of the tale itself, sounds suspiciously like devices used by Poe in "The Purloined Letter." Purloined, indeed!

Favorites: In 1927 Doyle published in the March issue of the Strand Magazine his twelve favorite Holmes stories, drawn from all but the stories to be published as *The Casebook of Sherlock Holmes*. SCAN is in fifth place on his list.

Vocabulary: Bohemian - unconventional (used to describe Holmes).

iodoform - a light yellow crystalline compound used as an antiseptic.

incognito - unknown; in disguise (from the Italian).

carte blanche - unrestricted authority (from the French).

bijou - jewel or trinket (used figuratively to describe a villa in this story; from the French).

ostler - a groom or stableboy.

"THE RED-HEADED LEAGUE"

The profile of Holmes comes into sharper focus in this story: the detective, eccentric, musician, and man of action. Cognizant of his abilities (he did not consider modesty a virtue), he utters the first of many complacent remarks. When Watson asks, "Holmes, what did you see?" He answers: "What I expected to see." He goes out of his way to impress Watson with feigned ignorance before revealing a lengthy string of deductions (which he terms "obvious" ones) about Wilson. (Find a parallel in STOC.)

Traits: More pronounced than ever are the character traits soon to be well known: boredom with humdrum routine; keen senses; sharp deductive faculties; a taciturn nature and reticence to discuss investigations; ability to concentrate matched by an ability to detach himself and turn his undivided attention to another pastime, such as music.

Cards: Side interests begin to surface. What will become frequent allusions to card playing show up. To while away the time until the bank robbers show their hand, Holmes carries a deck of cards. (Nowhere in the Canon is he seen actually playing.) Card analogies occur in SPEC, GREE, CHAS, BRUC, ILLU, MAZA, and SHOS.

Quotations: Like his predecessor Dupin, Holmes sprinkles an occasional foreign quote along the way, translating for Watson or the reader. "Omne ignotum pro magnifico" is well understood by Watson: "Everything unknown passes for something wonderful" - until it is explained. With hindsight, Watson always has twenty-twenty vision. The French saying of Flaubert sums up this case and Holmes' philosophy: "L'homme c'est rien - l'oeuvre c'est tout" (The man is nothing, the work is everything.) Sherlockians would not agree.

Favoritism: Doyle rated this story second on his list of twelve favorites for the *Strand*. The well-achieved elements of mystery and suspense, intensified by Holmes' cryptic, taciturn nature, and the night vigil are balanced as in few other stories, with a marvelous element of humor in the character and narrative of Mr. Wilson. By giving the story such a humorous and wild beginning, Doyle skillfully leaves the reader unprepared for the sudden burst of action and for the serious crime to follow.

Characterization: Each character is well drawn: the pompous and amusing Jabez Wilson; the dangerous John Clay (fourth most dangerous man in London. The third remains forever anonymous with Moriarty and Moran in first and second place respectively). Clay's delusions of grandeur are pitiful. The bulldog Inspector Peter Jones seems to be the same as Athelney Jones in SIGN.

Any reader wishing to gain a passing acquaintance with the world's most famous detective in a single story would find it here. Many paragraphs deal with his eccentric habits, his dual nature (the poetic and contemplative mood sometimes pre-dominating); his love of art, especially music. Written long before Doyle tired of Holmes, this story blends swift-placed adventure and compelling characterization.

Tricks: The famous ploy to keep a man out of the way by paying him to copy an entire encyclopedia finds a counterpart in STOC.

Watson: The plot is so clever that few would fail to sympathize with Watson when he says: "I was always oppressed with a sense of my own stupidity in my dealings with Sherlock Holmes."

Vocabulary: Albert Chain - a heavy metal watch chain named for Prince Albert, husband of Queen Victoria.

at scratch - from the very beginning.

crib - an easy berth or position.

press - a shelved cupboard or a case.

footpath - British for sidewalk.

stalls - theater seats nearest the orchestra on the ground floor.

rubber - a game of whist or bridge.

smasher - a person who passes counterfeit money.

bracelets - handcuffs.

crack a crib - break into a building.

partie carree - a party of four (French).

derbies - handcuffs.

"A CASE OF IDENTITY"

Although Holmes will label this one of the "innocent" cases he has handled, sometimes the very stories that involve no legal crimes prove to be the most heinous. (Tampering with a woman's affections is no slight matter.)

Chronologically, CASE succeeds SCAN by a few months because Watson has not yet seen the handsome gold snuffbox (Did Holmes' sniff?) sent by the King of Bohemia as a token of gratitude for Holmes' services. Watson begins what will become a habit: referring to past cases and alluding to some which are unrecorded. The reader is left to infer that the narrator is being selective and will record only the most extraordinary cases.

Victim-Villain: For the first but not the last time, the victim and villain are the identical person (St. Clair, MANW; Oldacre, NORW). This is the first of several cases where inheritance is the motive behind the crime (COPP, SPEC, SOLI).

Methods: Holmes displays his famous courtesy to client, Miss Mary Sutherland. His chivalry will be put to the test by others, especially Violet Smith (SOLI) who interrupts his concentration in an important case. Watson, Mary, and the reader are astonished by his amazing deductions, but he is not jealous of his secrets: "I always look first at a woman's sleeve; with a man, I observe the knees of his trousers." (In REDH trouser-knees indicate a digging job beneath a bank.)

Typewriters play an important part. The fact that Mary makes a modest living by typing, at a time when women were just venturing into the business world, gives insight into her character. Holmes' sleuthing involves analysis of typewritten notes and not a single one of sixteen distinct features of the machine escapes his notice. The stepfather's machinations are ended.

Maxims: Doyle beautifully envelops this story in maxims. The initial one, "life is infinitely stranger than anything the mind of man could invent," compels the reader to find out how it will be illustrated. Watson proves the attentive amanuensis who records each and every wise saying as it falls from the lips of the Master. Perhaps the most Holmesian aphorism concerns the symptoms of women who call for help. "Oscillation upon the pavement always means an affaire de coeur." He then wryly concludes that when a woman has been wronged by a man, the bell wire will have to be repaired.

Mary: That the reader is left wondering what will become of the young lady testifies to the fact that characterization is not lacking, although the ending is. She returns to live with a stepfather who, Holmes predicts, will rise from crime to crime until he reaches the gallows. Mary's gullibility may require an extra generous suspension of disbelief, but Doyle did prepare the reader when Holmes emphasized her poor eyesight by calling attention to an unmatched pair of shoes. Mary consulted Holmes without her father's permission, which indicates an independent spirit. Perhaps it was this combination in her character, plus Holmes' low estimate of a woman's intelligence guiding her love life, that leads him to caution Watson against telling Mary the truth. He backs his decision, to the dismay of many, with a Persian proverb: "There is danger for him who takes the tiger cub, and danger also for whoso snatches a delusion from a woman."

For the time being, Holmes can avoid taking such action. But do see ILLU.

Vocabulary: affaire de coeur - love affair (French).

voilá tout - that's all (French).

denouement - the unraveling or solution.

"THE BOSCOMBE VALLEY MYSTERY"

The first story to open on a domestic note at the Watson breakfast table is interrupted by a telegram from Holmes. A cursory glance at Mrs. Watson (Mary Morstan of SIGN) finds a gentle disposition early in the morning. At first, it seems incongruous that she who was concerned about her husband's paleness should encourage him to accompany Holmes when their cases occasionally warrant Watson's carrying a pistol. Undoubtedly, her suggestion is a tribute to the confidence she has in Holmes and in the value of their friendship. No sign of jealousy or resentment is present.

Footprints: What looked like an open and closed case of parricide eventually proves Holmes' paradox about how a simple case can prove extremely difficult. The art of deduction is exhibited methodically, and groundwork is laid for the importance of footprints and the amount of information they provide.

Monographs: Holmes' uncanny knowledge of cigars and tobacco ash is the result of a monograph written on the subject in which he identified one hundred and fourteen varieties. Other monographs include two on the human ear (CARD), ciphers (DANC), tattoos (REDH and MUSG), and the polyphonic motets of Lassus (BRUC). On several occasions, he mentions a desire to write one: In CASE, he considers writing on the relation between typewriters and crime, in LION, on dogs.

The Weapon: Holmes always discovers the weapon and this case is no exception. It is a case of his not leaving a stone unturned.

Compassion: The fact that Holmes does not hand the murderer over to the police is not so much a question of sympathy for the criminal as it is a total lack of sympathy for blackmailers who in his opinion get their just desserts, sometimes outside of the law. Holmes is more willing to let nature take its course in this case because the offender is a dying man (also a diabetic). He leaves him to the verdict of a higher court, which implies Holmes' belief in an afterlife and a final judgment. (Doyle was educated as a Roman Catholic, but gave up his faith about the time he entered medical school.)

Medical Knowledge: Despite the fact that Doyle was a physician, he rarely made use of his knowledge in these stories. Not only are his criminals fully responsible for their actions, but sympathy is never elicited on the score of disease.

Quotations: Interest in the story itself is subsidiary to the opening and conclusion of it. Doyle frequently has Watson sum up a story with one of the Master's apt comments, original or borrowed. Doyle credits Baxter with the profound sentiment: "There but for the grace of God goes (Sherlock Holmes)." Of all the men to whom the original form of this sentence is attributed, including Bunyan and Bradford, the man whose spirit is epitomized by it is Philip Neri (1515-1594, a contemporary of Bradford), founder of the Oratorian Fathers.

Petrarch: Why does Doyle go out of his way to have Holmes mention his Pocket Petrarch? To impress readers with his culture? To hint that he was reading an Italian version (for the reader's preparation for REDC)?

Hunting Terms: In at least four stories, Doyle shows himself familiar with hunting terms: BOSC, DANC, BRUC, DEVI.

Details: A multiplicity of details, inductions, and deductions makes Watson's review of this case tedious reading, although the effort of Doyle was to focus in on the story and provide hypotheses.

Vocabulary: métier - trade or profession (French).

outré - strikingly odd or exaggerated (French).

yellow-backed novel - a cheap popular novel, formerly printed between yellow covers.

George Meredith - English novelist and poet (1828-1909).

Nous verrons - We shall see (French).

"THE FIVE ORANGE PIPS"

Several unusual features characterize this case in which the intrepid Holmes pits himself against members of the Ku Klux Klan, knowing full well that few men braved the KKK's threats with impunity. For the first time, Holmes fails to prevent a tragedy from befalling a client, but it will happen once more in DANC to Hilton Cubitt.

Title: Doyle uses bland titles for his stories with the exception of this one and perhaps REDH, SPEC, SUSS, and 3GAR.

Emotion: A client is murdered after consulting Holmes, and never has Watson seen his friend so ruffled. The cool intellectual displays momentarily his intense emotion, of which he is usually a stern master. Wounded pride and remorse give way to a passionate desire to avenge his client's death and bring the criminals to justice.

Suspense: The story tends to be slow-moving as the result of lengthy exposition. A story within a story unfolds as John Openshaw sketches a background of relentless persecution by the KKK. Suspense is achieved and heightened by the repetition of having three individuals receive the pips one at a time, watching their frantic terror, and witnessing a fatal catastrophe in each case.

Atmospheric Effects: Capitalizing on atmospheric effects, Doyle employs weather conditions beautifully. A wild story unfolds on a night when London was hit by one of the wildest storms in its history. For a client to arrive in the midst of it indicates how desperate he is. The fury of the natural elements not only foreshadows the outcome but makes Openshaw's death seem accidental to the police. The conclusion of the storm and of Openshaw's life seems to dovetail the way details of the French detective author, Gaboriau, often did. Realism is maintained by the way that Doyle leaves many details unknown to Holmes.

Watson: Watson, acknowledged by Holmes as his only friend, serves in his usual capacity of the common man. In answering a socratic questioning, he serves to assemble the clues as far as the average man could, and then the Master Mind cracks the mystery. The only item of which the Master seems ignorant is the identity of the Lone Star State.

Vocabulary: carpet-bag politicians: Northern politicians who exploited weaknesses of the South after the American Civil War.

"THE MAN WITH THE TWISTED LIP"

This is the third of fifteen crimeless stories and the first case of a lost and found husband. (Women seem more eager to recover fiances.) It belongs in the category of CASE and NORW in that the apparent victim emerges as the villain.

The Opium Den: Atmospheric effects are marvelous as Watson makes his way through the vilest sections of London and the opium den, The Bar of Gold. There, ensues one of the best encounters of the immortal pair. Repulsed by a "decrepit old man," Watson is ordered to pass and then look back - only to find Holmes with a "fancy meeting you here" smile. On a par with this meeting is the one in DISA; superior to both is that of EMPT when Watson faints at the sight of what he thinks is Holmes' ghost.

Disguise: Professional disguises are at the heart of this matter. One disguise artist lays another bare by washing his face. (The make-up so quickly applied is as easily removed!) St. Clair's exposure constitutes one of the most dramatic in the Canon. To reach his conclusion, Holmes keeps an all night vigil, a spectacle of a mind at work. (If he had a "three pipe problem" in REDH and needed fifty minutes, one wonders how many he smoked through the night.)

Names: Doyle makes Holmes' world a man's world, but the wives in this story raise interesting questions. Watson's wife, be it first or second, calls him "James" instead of John or even Jack. Many interesting theories have resulted. Was James a former lover or husband? Is Dorothy Sayers correct in proposing that Watson's middle initial (H) is the Gaelic, Hamish, which in turn becomes James in English? (Is that begging the question?) Perhaps it is an insight into a woman with an affectionate nature who enjoys calling her husband James because he was the James Boswell to Holmes. Or is this one of Doyle's rogueries? Nomenclature was definitely not his forte. His favorite name for women is certainly Violet (COPP, SOLI, BRUC, ILLU); of four named dogs, two are Carlo; there are no less than sixteen Jameses in the Canon with three stories containing two: BLUE, BLAN, PRIO. Both Moriarty Brothers are named James!

Dialogue: The clipped dialogue is excellent and when Watson discovers Holmes, their conversation verges on stichomythia (rapid exchange of lines in Greek drama).

Curiosity: Critics may find fault with Holmes for "not playing fair" with the reader when he keeps his hunches to himself. This withholding, however, piques curiosity. When Holmes calls himself a fool who deserves to be kicked all the way to Charing Cross, he makes the reader more impatient to see the light.

Unlikelihoods: What seems unlikely is that Inspector Bradstreet would not perceive the disguise worn by the prisoner who refused to wash for days; that Holmes, himself an artist, should take so long to penetrate it; that it would take two wipes of the face to awaken the prisoner; and that the make-up would vanish so quickly.

Forfeit: What a chance Doyle forfeited when he had Holmes merely relate how clever and witty the beggar Boone was, when one good example would have done wonders. The writer's craft can be skillfully exhibited by showing instead of telling. A little humor would have been a welcome addition.

Vocabulary: slop shop - a store selling goods to sailors.

mousseline-de-soie - muslin-like silk fabric (French).

Gladstone bag - a small leather traveling bag popularized by Prime Minister Gladstone.

"THE BLUE CARBUNCLE"

Remarkable both for its surprise ending and unusual display of Holmes' deductive reasoning, this is the first of several cases to deal with the theft of a precious jewel (BERY, SIXN). Holmes places it in the same category as SCAN, CASE, and MANW, calling it a "whimsical problem." The setting is Christmas, December 27 to be exact, which certainly justifies the ending.

Bait: When Holmes tells Watson that good stones are the devil's bait, he not only produces a good **metaphor** but describes the very method he will use to trace, in reverse, the path of the carbuncle or garnet: bait. Beginning with his favorite, the newspaper ad, he has a humorous encounter with the owner of the most famous black hat in literature, Henry Baker. Never from so little was so much information drawn. One by one the innocent parties are crossed off the list on this wild goose chase. The Master's knowledge of human nature guides him to use the bait of a wager to obtain information from an irate goose keeper who could not have been bribed by any amount of money, but who could not resist a bet for anything.

Humor And Compassion: Holmes' taunting provides humor for the reader, especially when Breckinridge addresses him as "Mr. Cocksure." (He'll be "Mr. Busybody" in SOLI.) Watson notes that on leaving the shop, Holmes laughed in the hearty, noiseless fashion that was peculiar to him. The culprit turns out to be a first offender, a Peter Lorre-type. Holmes reasons that in letting him go, he may be committing a felony but he might possibly be saving a soul. For similar leniency in more serious cases, see CHAR and ABBE. Christopher Morley marvels at the perfect attitude of this "Christmas story without slush."

Tone: Doyle's light-hearted tone in this story sets it apart from most of the others with the exception of REDH and 3GAR. These do not have an ending in keeping with their tone. The ending for BLUE is appropriate because Christmas is "the season of forgiveness."

Solecisms: Critics bicker about all the possible deductions that could have been drawn from the identical clues that Holmes worked with on the black hat. They also insist there is no such thing as a blue carbuncle. They point out that Holmes' dressing gown was not purple, but mouse-colored in the past. (Could he not have owned two?) Such details subtract little from an enjoyable treasure hunt, sweeping detectives and reader through London's vast panorama. Minor characters produce in the reader the quiet laughter indulged in by the sleuth himself.

Sherlockismus: In 1927 Father Ronald Knox coined this term for a Holmesian epigram. He refers readers to Ratzegger who collected over one hundred and sixty-three of them. In this story, Holmes introduces himself: "My name is...Holmes. It is my business to know what other people do not know." For other famous examples, see REDH, SILV, NAVA.

Vocabulary: "Pink Un" - a Victorian sporting journal printed on pink paper.

billycock - a low - crowned felt hat; also, a bowler or derby.

Assizes - one of the regular court sessions held in each county in England for the trial of civil and criminal cases by jury.

disjecta membra - scattered limbs (Latin).

"THE SPECKLED BAND"

For sheer suspense, eerie atmosphere, mystery, a blackguard of a villain, and a colorful Holmes, this story is peerless.

Bully Treatment: On Miss Stoner's departure, her stepfather intrudes and, in a peak of anger, threatens Holmes by bending a poker with his bare hands. Unintimidated, Holmes bends the poker back to its original position (more a feat than the first performance). Watson's admiration makes up for the lack of other witnesses. Holmes would never stoop to using his physical strength as a threat.

Suspense: Doyle's use of suspense, as Holmes and Watson wait in the dark for they know not what, is incomparable in the Canon. With his cane, Holmes strikes out at what he learns is a deadly snake, from which the story takes its title. Meant for Miss Stoner, the snake recoils; its owner is dead by the time Holmes and Watson reach him.

The Snake: The snake is a widely discussed item. Ophiologists assert that no snake drinks milk, has the ability to climb a rope, or can hear a whistle. Although no snake conforms completely to Doyle's description, the cobra comes closest for color and movement. The rapidity of the venom's effect on Dr. Roylott leads many to suspect that his death occurred from apoplexy.

Number One: This was Doyle's favorite story, a preference shared by many Sherlockians. It is an archetype of perfect Holmesian construction. The clues are fairly well laid out for the reader with even a red herring thrown in by the twin sister's dying words, "Speckled Band" misleading Holmes and readers to an association with neighborhood gypsies.

Characterization: Dr. Grimsby-Roylott is one of the most vivid characters to enliven the pages of The Adventures. Doyle uses restraint effectively when the girl declines to explain the nature of the livid fingerprints on her wrist. The build-up for his entrance has no let down when he does appear. Holmes was right: When a doctor turns evil, he is a dangerous criminal because he has nerve and knowledge. Fortunately for his daughter, he meets his match in Holmes who is blase about his part in the man's death. And the cool humor displayed by Holmes before the irate Roylott is Holmes at his best. The man's strength made him an imposing and formidable foe, but his violent temper and lack of foresight change him from a calculating criminal to a blustering bully.

Plot: Undoubtedly, this is one of the superior plots with numerous clues, suspense, an exciting **denouement**, and no loose ends.

"THE ENGINEER'S THUMB"

Few stories compare with this one in portraying the compassion of Watson and Holmes for a wounded man needing the assistance of a doctor and a detective. Similar concern is shown to John Turner, a diabetic in BOSC, and to Percy Phelps who suffered from brain fever in NAVA.

Gothicism: Like 3GAR, this is at bottom a counterfeit-detection plot, but the tone of the two stories is diametrically opposed. This Gothic thriller has the Romantic trapping of a foreign villain (who lapses into English right at the climax!), utmost secrecy to the point of pirating the engineer off in the dead of night in a carriage with frosted windows to a hideout. (In GREE another man's skill will be needed by criminals and the windows will be covered with paper.) Hatherley is trapped inside a hydraulic press to be crushed by a descending ceiling - a descendant of Poe's "Pit and the Pendulum."

One harrowing escape is followed immediately by another - being chased by a madman wielding a butcher's cleaver. Granted, readers realize the young man will live to tell his tale; still, they are well aware and in dread of the incident that will cost him his thumb.

The Listener: Holmes is an excellent listener and when he interrupts, especially with a formal apology, as he does here to ask about the horse, it is fair warning of an important clue. Of course, its significance is lost on the average reader. Holmes qualifies as the man on whom nothing is lost.

Scotland Yard: Working with Inspector Bradstreet and four constables, Holmes proves that even five heads are not better than one when that one belongs to him. Four men give reasons for suspecting the location of the hiding place, each choosing a different point on the compass. Holmes' quiet assertion, "I think I could lay my finger on it" is, in effect, explosive. To make it more ironic, the Inspector concludes that one of his men must be correct; with whom does Holmes agree? The stroke of genius levels all four theories, locating the site dead center with irrefutable logic.

Melodrama: Technically, the hair-breadth adventures are sheer melodrama, but Doyle uses two strategies to make them more credible. The first is a lengthy introduction in the realistic surroundings of Watson's home and then the familiar 221B Baker Street. The second is Holmes' assurance to the dejected engineer that for the rest of his life he will have a first-hand experience with which to enthrall his listeners.

Deus Ex Machina: Hatherley's escape from the machine is literally a **deus ex machina** but, since it does not benefit the detective, it is less offensive in terms of contrivance. (**Deus ex machina**: a device used in Greek drama to resolve the situation by lowering a "god" onto the stage. Literally "god" from a machine and figuratively an unbelievably providential rescue from danger, it applies to the plight of Hatherley, whose rescuer actually appeared from a machine.)

Hatherley: The engineer emerges a character in his own right. Despite irregular proceedings and a sympathetic woman's entreaties to flee for his life, he is determined to see the project through. Facing a violent death, he coolly reasons about which position would be less painful and decides against a supine one in order to avoid snapping the spinal column. His calm nature is well documented, but the indication of his aesthetic nature is out of place in the context of running from a butcher and stopping to admire the garden before leaping. In retrospect, this might be appropriate recall, but not under the actual circumstances.

Vocabulary: fuller's earth - a soft, absorbent material resembling clay.

"THE NOBLE BACHELOR"

If an American reader's **connotation** of the adjective in the title leads to ambiguity, it will lead also to disappointment. Lord St. Simon may be a noble, but he is definitely not noble. In fact, he is rather pompous which guarantees humor when he comes into contact with deflating Holmes.

Wit: Holmes' pungent wit is exercised to the full. On receiving the noble's envelope with crest and monogram, he fears it will prove to be one of those invitations that "call upon a man either to be bored or to lie." When St. Simon presumes that the detective is not accustomed to drawing clients from his class of society, Holmes squelches him with: "My last client of the sort was a king." The bachelor almost seems disappointed when Holmes solves the case from his armchair (as in CASE and REDH). When St. Simon suggests it will take wiser heads than his or Holmes' to locate his missing bride, Holmes makes a pretense of being highly honored to have his head on the same level as the noble's. The latter seems unruffled by sarcasm.

St. Simon: The noble bachelor is left the picture of wounded dignity even after his bride produces her first husband. The word "bigamy" is never mentioned.

Logic: Doyle placed this story low on his list, but it does have its merits in places. For example, when Inspector Lestrade argues that the woman's body must be in the river because her bridal gown was found there, Holmes carries that premise to its logical conclusion: "By the same brilliant reasoning, every man's body is to be found" near his wardrobe. For a parallel lesson in syllogisms, see BOSC where Holmes accuses the inspector of giving a suspect credit for both too much imagination and too little.

Vocabulary: tide-waiter - a customs officer who boards vessels entering port, to enforce customs regulations.

danseuse - a female professional dancer; a ballet girl (French).

fait accompli - an accomplished fact; a thing done and irrevocable (French).

pea-jacket - a short coat of thick woolen cloth, worn by seamen (and by Holmes in SIGN and REDH).

paté de foie gras - a paste of fat goose liver (French).

"THE BERYL CORONET"

This tale presents another example of Holmes' professional instincts refusing to accept the obvious facts of the case as conclusive. A chain of events which leads the others to one answer points in the opposite direction for Holmes, as did the thumbprint in NORW.

The Client: Obviously, Alexander Holder is unstable and unfit for the grave responsibilities of his position. His decision to take the valuable coronet home for safekeeping rather than leave it in the well-protected bank; his placing it in a cupboard which "any old key can open"; and his discussion of its location in the presence of his family and servants all prove his foolishness. Nor is he less foolish in rejoicing at the return of the missing stones because his client had warned him that any injury would be almost as serious as its complete loss. How did he expect to mend the coronet in time to return it?

Payment: This is one of the rare cases in which Holmes accepts a large fee for his services. He actually demands a reward from the Duke of Holdernesse in PRIO, as punishment for the Duke's deceit. Here, his motivation could have been to teach the foolish Holder an object lesson.

Identity: There is little doubt among Sherlockians that Holder's "illustrious client" was Albert Edward, Prince of Wales to whom Watson refers in ILLU with the same identical phrase. As Duke of Rothesay, Edward would be the legitimate keeper of a duke's coronet.

Conjecturing: Holmes' love of conjecture is evident here. Speaking to Holder about his son, Holmes says: "He conducted himself in this matter as I should be proud to see my own son do, should I ever...have one." Notice how Holmes conjectures about possible love in DEVI, and about a possible daughter in ILLU.

Some commentators have used BERY as a basis to speculate that Holmes actually did sire a son (by Irene Adler?). Guesses as to his identity include Inspector Stanley Hopkins (BLAC) for whom Holmes shows such a paternal friendliness; Dorothy Sayer's detective Lord Peter Wimsey; and Rex Stout's Nero Wolfe (whose temperament is similar to Mycroft's - see GREE and EMPT).

Construction: While the story is a good mystery, it moves slowly because of lengthy narratives at the beginning and the end. What little action there is, is reported secondhand. The story is another good example, though, of typical Holmes construction: opening at 221B; entrance of distressed client; presentation of case; investigation of the scene of the crime and suspects; climactic revelation of the truth and anticlimactic explanation of deductions.

Opening: Doyle uses an intriguing opening (with Holmes declaring that a madman is coming down the street) to catch the reader's attention. Holder's entrance ranks with those of McFarlane (NORW), Huxtable (PRIO), and Steve Dixie (3GAB).

"THE COPPER BEECHES"

In the opening paragraphs, readers discover not only what Holmes really thinks of Watson's writings, but also one of the best personality sketches of the Master (second only to REDH). Fully revealed are his likes, dislikes, and reactions. He has a distaste for emotion; he has occasional fits of depression and cynicism brought on by boredom with the lack of imagination in both police and criminals alike; he has a love for his work and art. He reprimands his chronicler: "You have degraded what should have been a course of lectures into a series of tales." His excuse for this reproach is that sensational crime is commonplace but true logic is rare.

Experience: Holmes' attitude towards Watson and his narrative art will be tempered somewhat when Holmes tries his own hand at writing BLAN and LION, both romanticized.

Violet Hunter: She is one of the most sensible and capable young ladies in the Canon. She holds the distinction of being the only woman after Irene Adler for whom Holmes manifests any non-business interest. At first, he refers to her sneeringly; but soon Watson detects that Holmes is impressed by her. Holmes shows a brotherly affection for her and by the end of the story feels that she is brave, sensible, and exceptional. High praise indeed from such a seeming misogynist! The interest was not one-sided, for Violet confesses that she lay awake half the night thinking about Holmes. Romantic Watson is disappointed that Holmes manifests no further interest in Violet.

Parallelism: As early as this twelfth story, Doyle was tiring of Holmes. Perhaps Holmes' reprimand to Watson at the beginning is a manifestation of Doyle's anger at himself for what he considered wasting valuable time on a series of tales which kept him from his more serious endeavors. Doyle, too, wanted "justice for his art."

Inspiration: It was Doyle's mother who temporarily saved Holmes from assassination; she begged her son to write a story about a girl with beautiful golden hair who was kidnapped and, her hair shorn, was made to impersonate another girl for a villainous purpose.

Craft: In a highly suspenseful story, Doyle makes use of one of his favorite tricks: progressing from a trivial beginning to a sinister climax for which the reader is unprepared. Step by step, Violet's position becomes more threatening until the final confrontation between hero and villain. The culminating events, although catering to public taste for the sensationally gruesome, are exciting. Although Doyle was tiring of Holmes, the story shows no sign of it in the well-defined characterization and philosophies of Holmes. The ending, in which the eventual fates of all are recounted, is typically Dickensian and Victorian.

Vocabulary: misogynist - a woman-hater.

THE MEMOIRS OF SHERLOCK HOLMES

"SILVER BLAZE"

This tale is typical of the dry English "puzzle" school of mystery writing, and is probably the classic Holmesian puzzle. It contains little of the bizarre or unusual found in so many cases, and a good deal is presented in rather dry narrative fashion (notably Holmes' opening review of the case and his anticlimactic explanation of the crime at the end); but despite this lack of excitement, it is a well-planned and baffling mystery. All clues are presented fairly, and there is a classic "red herring" in the form of the falsely accused tout, Simpson.

Sherlockismus: Besides its other virtues, this story contains one of the most oft-quoted and classic examples of what Ronald Knox termed the "Sherlockismus": namely the dialogue about "the curious incident of the dog in the night-time." This is the reticent, dramatic, and baffling Holmes. The device of the dog that failed to bark because it recognized the villain will be used by other writers.

Bullies: This tale offers Holmes ample opportunity to deal with bullies and stuffed-shirts in the persons of Ross and Brown. He allows the pompous, skeptical Colonel Ross to worry about the horse's recovery for a sufficient time before stripping Silver

Blaze's disguise. (Compare to his treatment of Percy Phelps in NAVA or Lord Cantlemere in MAZA.)

Plot Tricks: As well as resurrecting certain basic character types in the Holmes stories, Doyle sometimes lifted plot tricks from one story to another, e.g., Jacky's experimentation with poison on the dog in SUSS, which forms an obvious parallel with the sheep in SILV.

In Command: So obvious is Holmes' confidence and control of the situation that the story lacks real excitement or suspense; yet the intriguing intellectual challenge, complete with fair clues and red herring, provides more than adequate compensation for any reader.

Wager: While in the mood of the story, Doyle bet his wife that she could not guess the identity of the murderer. Although there is no documentation, it is unlikely that he lost.

Criticism: Doyle was taken to task for the solecisms (deviations from the accepted order) that marred this story for some experts. He admitted that his ignorance of the turf cried aloud to heaven and he gave credit to an expert who wrote an "excellent and very damaging criticism." The embarrassment Doyle experienced must account for his omitting this story from his list of favorites, although fans place it high on theirs. (Ellery Queen insists it belongs among the top five Holmes stories.)

Memoirs: SILV introduced the second series of Holmes stories published in the *Strand* (December 1892) which were later collected under the title *The Memoirs of Sherlock Holmes*.

"THE YELLOW FACE"

This story does not involve Holmes with much of a challenge. It begins as a marital problem and ends with a family solution, with the immortal pair serving as good listeners and witnesses. Grant Munro ("Jack" to his wife), concerned about his wife's inexplicable behavior, sounds like Hilton Cubitt in DANC, only this case has a happy ending. Both men married widows from America who kept a secret which the men would have been better off knowing. Munro also resembles Phelps of NAVA because in describing their predicament, both men call on God as well as Holmes for help.

Pipes: Holmes performs feats of deduction on the pipe left by Munro: few things possess "more individuality." Unlike later sleuths, Holmes does not solve any mystery by noting dental irregularities.

Children: The child in this story acts as a catalyst. In only three other stories does Doyle employ children, although in several the client is a governess. In DANC, the child never appears, but the fact that St. Clair had promised to bring home a toy leads his wife to conclude from the sight of a toy in the opium den that her husband had been there. In PRIO, the disappearance of Lord Saltire is the raison d'etre for the case. In SUSS, the youth is actually the villain. In COPP, Holmes confided that he frequently gained understanding of the character of parents by studying their children.

Denouement: Doyle's denouement is both melodramatic and anticlimactic. It is hard to credit a deliberation that would last ten whole minutes uninterrupted by four persons. The best part of the story is the ending when Holmes whispers to Watson a word that should be proof against pride forever: "Norbury" (the name of the estate). There is no record of Watson's ever using it.

> Vocabulary: a brown wide-awake - a soft, broad-brimmed felt hat.
>
> hop merchant - seller of wooden troughs through which grain passes into a mill.
>
> Crystal Palace - a glass building constructed by John Paxton for the Great Exhibition in 1851 at Hyde Park.
>
> catalyst - an agent that remains unaltered while inducing great disturbances around him (or it).

"THE STOCKBROKER'S CLERK"

This rather unremarkable case offers little in the way of deduction or suspense until the final memorable scene. However, the opening paragraphs do give the reader a pleasant, intimate view of Watson's married life with Mary Morstan (of SIGN fame) and his newly purchased practice. It is convenient for Watson that both his wife and his neighbor are of an understanding nature, thereby enabling him to take off upon an adventure with Holmes at a moment's notice.

Client: A remarkable feature of the case is Holmes' client, Mr. Hall Pycroft. Surely Holmes has had few clients as entertaining, down-to-earth, pleasant, and intelligent. Although he condemns himself as a "soft Johnny" and a "blind beetle" it is clear that he is, on the contrary, a bright and likable young man. He says that he is not very good at "telling a story"; yet, he proves himself to be admirably lucid as well as entertaining, far superior to Holmes as narrator (see BLAN and LION). Not only was Pycroft observant enough to notice that both of the Pinner brothers had the same gold-filled tooth, he also had a sharp enough intellect to memorize the price of major stocks on a day-to-day basis.

Panorama: The story also presents a panoramic view of England, especially the financial England of the day, as Pycroft's narrative and Holmes' journey carry the reader from the financial section of London to Pycroft's diggings in Hampstead, then away from London to another important financial city, Birmingham.

Similarities: Anyone familiar with the Canon will certainly notice the striking resemblance of the plot to that of REDH. Another seemingly absurd situation (a young man is hired for the trivial job of copying names from a phone book, just as Jabez Wilson was hired to copy the Encyclopedia Britannica) turns out to be a ploy to keep them away from something else. Doyle will use the idea again in 3GAR, having a man lured away from his house by another laughable hoax.

Execution: Although the plot is not entirely original, its execution is. Doyle shows a fine eye for characterization through dialogue, especially in his use of Cockney slang through Pycroft's narrative ("crib" for job; "screw" for salary, etc.). He also handles the element of suspense in the final scene masterfully. When Holmes, Pycroft, and Watson break into the room to which Pinner has supposedly flown, they find no one; this greatly heightens the suspense. Both **protagonists** and reader know that something dreadful is happening to Pinner but they know neither what nor where; they feel helpless to prevent it. Suspense builds to an unbearable point as they frantically search the room for Pinner. Even when they discover the closet in which he is trapped, Doyle draws out the suspense by using rhythmic phrases to slowly draw the reader's attention to the dying Pinner, rather than revealing him all at once. This passage reads almost like poetry, and is so much more effective than: "They found Pinner hanging in the closet"! Holmes' philosophical musing on human nature makes a satisfying ending.

"THE GLORIA SCOTT"

This case is not distinguished for the part Holmes plays in it, a very minimal one, but for the fact that it represents his very first case and the moment when he considered making a profession of his "merest hobby" of deduction.

College: Holmes' trifling part consists of witnessing the events and deciphering an extremely simple code letter, an action which in no way advances the story. Yet, there are interesting details of Holmes' college days: early on, he was a loner engaged in scientific research and developing his own techniques. Evidently, he was also fairly well off, for he could afford "London rooms" as well as those at the University (The eternal question is "Oxford or Cambridge?").

Reminiscence: Holmes is rarely communicative about his cases; but occasionally his love of the dramatic and desire for praise show through his detached facade and he invited Watson to publish a certain case or just to listen to him reminisce. Holmes is far better as a story-teller than as story-writer. (His two attempts at writing, LION and BLAN, are oddly romantic in style, unlike the tight-lipped Holmes who narrates GLOR.)

Hudson: It is to be hoped that the odious blackmailer, Hudson, is no relation to Holmes' long-suffering landlady.

Story-Within-A-Story: As in VEIL, YELL, and SOLI, Holmes' presence here is almost superfluous. As an adventure tale, this holds together nicely without the usual deductions. Doyle is fond of the "story within a story," such as the mutiny aboard the "Gloria Scott". He uses this retrospective device most notably in two novels, *A Study in Scarlet* and *The Valley of Fear*, in which his preference for historical fiction makes itself known as he ties together the deductive tale with a historical narrative by a slender plot thread. It also appears in FIVE, CROO, BLAC, and CARD where victim or villain have some explaining to do. In the "confessional retrospections," it is interesting to note how many have a nautical element. In this instance, both plot-lines are interesting and Doyle is in good form with the characterizations of J. P. Trevor, Pendergast, and the brief glimpse of Hudson.

Fainting: Doyle uses the dramatic device of fainting in several occasions in the saga. Three of the situations prove to be doubly effective because it is a man who swoons. Here, Holmes' deductive powers concerning Justice Trevor's past result in a dead faint, **foreshadowing** problems. In PRIO, the huge Dr. Huxtable faints; in EMPT, poor Watson collapses on seeing his long-lost friend come to life; in BLAN, the mother of Godfrey Emsworth faints from relief when she discovers her son is not a leper.

Vocabulary: callosity - a callus.

harness cask - a closed vessel containing salted meat to be used aboard ship.

knot - the speed of a nautical mile in an hour.

eight-knot tramp - a cargo steamer without regular ports of call or regular timetable, with a maximum speed of eight knots.

"THE MUSGRAVE RITUAL"

Without a doubt, the colorful personality of Holmes reaches the high-water mark at the outset of this story. Shooting a VR into his mantelpiece is not only highly British and patriotic, but the **episode** marks the zenith of his eccentricities. Even a second-rate story would have been famous appended to such an opening; however, the plots carry their own weight.

Reminiscences: Like GLOR, this story is a case of Holmes' reminiscing for Watson as he sorts his souvenirs at his friend's request to tidy up their living quarters. Holmes' career was launched in the former story by the need of an old classmate, and this third case results because another classmate needed his assistance.

Victim: The dismissed butler, Brunton, figures in two stories at the center of which is a treasure. The ritual, dating back to the days of the Stuarts, is recognized for what it is by Brunton. The puzzle is intriguing, and the fact that Brunton is one step ahead of Holmes costs him his life.

Solutions: Holmes and client, Musgrave, find the all-important answers but do not succeed in finding all of them. Unanswered is exactly how the butler met his death, the whereabouts of the maid, Rachel Howells, his accomplice and possibly vengeful murderer.

Understatement: Doyle provides real humor with Watson's use of understatement, complaining about Holmes' untidiness and queer humors. Incomparable is: "I felt strongly that neither the atmosphere nor the appearance of our room was improved by it" [the pistol practice].

Interest: Interest in the main plot is fostered by a good subplot. The puzzle element adds another dimension.

Verisimilitude is strained a little when Doyle asks the reader to believe that the royal crown of the Stuart Dynasty would remain in possession of a private family, regardless of how much they were willing to pay. Mr. Nathan Bengis has identified the crown as that of St. Edward, listed in the 1649 inventory.

Vocabulary: recherché - carefully selected (French).

café noir - black coffee (French).

billet - a short, thick stick as of firewood.

Cavalier - a supporter of Charles I of England; a Royalist.

"THE REIGATE PUZZLE"

A dramatic mystery, this tale begins in a manner similar to DEVI because Holmes must rest after his strong constitution breaks down in the course of a particularly rigorous investigation. He soon finds himself confronted by the very type of problem he sought to escape. There is something comical about Watson's attempts to keep Holmes inactive; always on the verge of succeeding, they are constantly thwarted by the appearance of a new piece of evidence.

Drama: The mystery may be called "dramatic" because Holmes' love of the dramatic manifests itself so many times. As in DYIN, Watson is pained to see the weakening effects of Holmes' illness - he errs when writing out the advertisement;

he knocks over a table and blames it on Watson, etc. Of course, the **denouement** reveals that each **episode** was conceived and executed by Holmes for a definite purpose. At the end he admits to concealing evidence in order to produce a more dramatic effect when the enlightenment came. Although he often resorts to unnecessarily dramatic tactics, he always explains them satisfactorily and honestly.

Handwriting: Experts have questioned Holmes' deduction of a man's age from his handwriting, as well as those "twenty-three other deductions" which he gleaned from the writing. Even were Holmes an expert graphologist, the first feat is impossible while the second is far-fetched.

Holmes And Doyle: This was twelfth on Doyle's "12 favorites" list and is certainly a swiftly paced mystery showing careful thought. Doyle often manages an extra touch of **realism** by leaving certain things (in this case, "the relations between Alec Cunningham, William Kirwan, and Annie Morrison") unexplained, something which few Victorian authors did. As Holmes is said to have done in his investigation of the Netherland-Sumatra Company, Doyle often worked more than fifteen hours a day in his writing.

Colonels: What did Doyle have against colonels? D. Martin Dakin, in his *A Sherlock Holmes Commentary*, points out that Colonel Hayter in this tale is perhaps the only respectable and pleasant colonel in the Canon. The list of unpleasant ones includes Moran (EMPT), Walters (BRUC), Barclay (CROO), Stark (ENGI), Moriarty (brother of the professor in FINA), Ross (SILV), and Carruthers (SOLI).

Title: There is an interesting history attached to the title. It first appeared as "The Reigate Squire" in the *Strand*. It was changed to "Squires" for the Memoirs. Its journey to America by way of *Harper's Weekly* saw the change from "Reigate Squires" to "Reigate Puzzle," lest democratic Americans not relish the term "squire."

"THE CROOKED MAN"

Watson receives his first visit as a married man from Holmes who shows off a bit, taking advantage of new surroundings to impress Watson that his powers of observation are never dormant. Their dialogue contains the memorable:

Excellent," I Cried.

Elementary," said he.

(This is not to be mistaken for the apocryphal "Elementary, my dear Watson.")

Practice: This rare visit of Holmes to Watson (repeated in STOC) involves a not-so-rare request: that Watson accompany him on a case. Watson seemingly has two helpful neighbor - doctors who will take his practice. Here it is Jackson; previously it was Anstruthers, unless Jackson is the Christian name of Anstruthers.

Names: Holmes solves this case by talking to the right people. The name "James" is again puzzling: this time because it was Not used by Mrs. Barclay for her husband of that name. The answer is one of the clues. She used "David" reproachfully, and Holmes' knowledge of Scripture, especially 2 Samuel, throws light on the subject. Nemesis occasions not murder by revenge but death through apoplexy.

Scripture: Doyle's use of the Bible is more integral in this story than elsewhere. He cleverly wove the **allusion** into the heart of his story, making Mrs. Barclay appear a very clever woman. His quotations are always appropriately applied. Alluding to the just punishment incurred by Baron Gruner in ILLU, he quotes half of Paul's words: "The wages of sin [is death], Watson..." (Romans 6,23). In DANC, the coded message warned, "Elsie, prepare to meet your God." The Prophet Amos said: "Israel, prepare to meet Thy God."

Baker Street Irregulars: This name was given to street urchins who ran errands and did small jobs for Holmes. Today it is the name of the celebrated stag society that meets every January to celebrate Holmes' birthday.

Mongoose: The red mongoose proves to be a red herring whose presence in the story seems a bit forced, little more than a diversion.

Vocabulary: florin - a British silver coin, equal to one-tenth of a pound or two shillings.

"THE RESIDENT PATIENT"

The title might lead the reader to expect Watson to play a major role as a physician, putting to good use Doyle's medical background. Instead, it is Holmes who displays his medical knowledge and detects a murder instead of an apparent suicide. The hanging man did not fare as well here as the one in STOC. Just like the KKK murders in FIVE, the guilty parties seeking revenge meet their deaths in an ill-fated ship. (Ships in general seem to be ill-fated in the Canon: Gloria Scott; Norah Creina; Friesland; Matilda Briggs; Alicia.)

Watson's Wound: The famous line by Holmes, "Your hand stole toward your old wound," leaves the reader to guess whether it pressed a shoulder or a leg. The chair in this story seems to support the leg. Watson spoke of being wounded by a jezail bullet on the shoulder which "shattered the bone and grazed the subclavian artery." In the SIGN, he spoke of a leg wound which did not prevent him from walking but ached in damp weather. In NOBL, he refers to a troublesome "limb." Readers are left with a bone or two of contention.

Mindreading: Readers of the Sherlock Holmes stories will find that the mindreading **episode** performed by Holmes on Watson (after the manner of Dupin) appears word for word in CARD. The explanation is that it belongs in the latter story where it first appeared. CARD was omitted from the Memoirs lest it offend Victorian taste with the illicit love affair. That **episode** was inserted into this story instead. By 1917 when the collected works appeared, CARD was included with the mindreading in its proper setting. American publishers left it in both stories. It might have served a more useful purpose as a prelude to this story because CARD would be just as interesting without it, whereas this story profits from a more interesting opening.

Details: Most of the clues in this story are rather trite, with the patient's feigning catalepsy the only novel feature. Mythological allusions figure rarely in Doyle but two occur here. He employed the figure of Hercules to describe the build of the King in SCAN; here it describes the Russian nobleman's companion. Watson terms his dilemma, in selecting which cases to record, a Scylla and Charybdis either Holmes plays an insignificant part in an exciting case or else Holmes is spectacular in a dull case.

Vocabulary: tour-de-force - a feat of remarkable strength or skill (French).

Scylla and Charybdis - sea monsters; the former had six heads which snatched sailors from ships; the latter sucked the ships into its whirlpool. Figuratively, they represent a dilemma: two perils where the avoidance of one leads to the dangers of the other.

"THE GREEK INTERPRETER"

This curious adventure appears to have been chronicled for the sole but noble purpose of introducing Holmes' brother, Mycroft, to the public. Seven years Sherlock's senior, Mycroft appears in only three stories (BRUC and FINA) but he has taken his place among the satellite figures like Moriarty and Irene Adler.

The Diogenes Club: Holmes takes Watson to meet his brother, a founder-member at the "queerest of clubs," the Diogenes Club. In short, it is an anti-clubbing Club for those who, "some from shyness, some from misanthropy, have no wish for the company of their fellows."

Mycroft: Sherlock's deductive powers are matched and surpassed in an entertaining piece of observational rivalry. Although superior to Sherlock in intellectual and deductive acumen, Mycroft lacks the physical energy and ambition for detective work. (What a pair they might have made!) Mycroft prefers to remain a humble government accountant, although it is revealed later (BRUC) that his position was not so modest.

The Tale: This weak-plotted story is just a good excuse for meeting Sherlock's nearest of kin. When Mycroft's research unearths the whereabouts of the kidnappers, he gives his energetic younger brother the legwork to do. Holmes and Watson appear in time to save one but not both of the victims. An occasional failure (see FIVE, DANC, ENGI) brings out Holmes' humanity and makes him more credible.

Characterization: Doyle's characterization saves a basically weak plot. His comparison and contrast between the brothers, rather than the usual mystery, forms the basis of the story. The quiet villain, Wilson Kemp, is superbly drawn: he speaks softly, giggles constantly, and frightens the victim more than his blustering accomplice does. The title character, Melas, is also memorable, but Holmes fails to shine. Someone else reveals the criminals' locations: incredible enough, Watson deduces the motives for the criminals' actions; and Holmes arrives too late to save the unfortunate Kratides.

Weaknesses: The translation scene between Melas and Kratides as well as the journey to the hiding place are suspenseful. But plot weaknesses are glaring. Why did the criminals take such a roundabout way of killing? It almost looks as though they were waiting for Holmes to rescue Melas. As for the newspaper clipping, let Mycroft take credit.

"THE NAVAL TREATY"

This last story before Doyle's nefarious attempt to kill Holmes in Fina clearly shows signs that Doyle was tiring of his creation. Holmes comes off well, but the story is over-long and marred by inconsistencies.

Objections: Curious incidents surround the treaty, let alone its disappearance. Why should an Anglo-Italian treaty be written in French? (Because it was the international language?) And why should an extra copy of it be done in longhand by Phelps when copying machines and typewriters were available at the time? (It almost seems as though Lord Holdhurst were guilty of nepotism and had to create jobs for his nephew to keep him on the payroll.) And surely no such building as pictured in the diagram could have existed, with corridors seemingly carved in solid rock - most unlike the Home Office of London which was supposedly represented. How could Harrison have realized the treaty's importance and escaped with it in the few seconds between the time he rang for Phelps and his arrival? And why, when Phelps collapsed with "brain fever," was he taken to Harrison's room instead of his own when they were both in the same house? The questions are legion.

Reflections: Holmes' reflective nature finds expression on several subjects. He waxes eloquent when he speaks of the English board schools as "lighthouses" He deduces the goodness of Providence from flowers, especially the rose. William S. Baring Gould notes that this is the only passage in the long Saga in which Holmes speaks forthrightly of religion.

Sherlockismus: Another famous example develops when Holmes tells Annie Harrison he suspects himself of something.

Methods: Holmes' love of the dramatic and his inscrutability are manifest. He tells no one of his reasons for remaining in Woking, and, consequently, his final revelations are more dramatic and effective. He indulges in a practical joke in the way he returns the treaty to Phelps. (Compare this with his treatment of Ross in SILV, Oldacre in NORW, and Cantlemere in MAZA.)

Combat: Harrison gives Holmes a good fight and had to be "grassed" (knocked down) twice. Verbally, he assaulted Holmes: "For a moment I thought you had done something clever." An interesting villain.

Client: Phelps is not so interesting a client. He tends to be weak and not just as the result of brain fever. This old classmate of Watson may well have been nicknamed "Tadpole."

Brain Fever: This malady, which also affected Susan Cushing (CARD), is now known as meningitis or even encephalitis, inflammation of the membranes of the brain. Recovery was rare, but both persons in the stories survived. The illness lasted for months, during which time the patient was not to be disturbed; he required around-the-clock nursing in a darkened, quiet room.

Marriage: Watson dates this story the July after his marriage. Critics are agreed that he refers to his first marriage with Mary Morstan whom he met during SIGN.

Ending: The story becomes somewhat tedious because there is so much narrative. The ending, however, is abrupt - almost as though Doyle tired of the whole thing and decided to finish it off quickly.

Vocabulary: wicket - in cricket, the object at which the bowler aims, comprising three upright rods and two small pieces lying in grooves along their tops.

chevy - British slang: to chase or harrass.

Triple Alliance - alliance formed among Germany, Austria-Hungary Hungary, and Italy in 1882.

Huguenots - French Calvinist Protestants.

"THE FINAL PROBLEM"

Intended to be the last story ever written about Holmes, this tale is one of the finest in the Canon.

Watson: Watson is depicted at his prosaic best. The sincerity of his grief at his friend's death and his admiration for Holmes seem to transcend the pages. A plethora of details, included so as to heighten the realism, serves to balance out Watson's occasional tendency toward emotional eulogy. Watson, the faithful standby, is loyal to the end: ready to fly at a moment's notice to the Continent, to risk his life and lose his luggage in serving Holmes. As a doctor and man of valor, Watson reaches the peak of his career when he leaves the side of his friend to travel miles in order to comfort a dying woman for whom he knows he can effect no cure.

Holmes: Holmes is also at his best - cool, logical, philosophical, but considerate. He is portrayed as the deep thinker, the profound philosopher, who calmly confronts death. His monologue is moving: "I think... I may go so far as to say... I have not lived wholly in vain... In over a thousand cases I am not aware that I have ever used my powers upon the wrong side." Surely that speech must stand as his epitaph.

Holmes' nonchalant attitude toward the loss of his only material possessions in the fire at his Baker Street rooms only emphasizes his readiness to give up the world for a good cause.

Moriarty: The "Napoleon of Crime" is the only Canonical criminal truly worthy of Holmes' full powers. No lesser villain could ever have brought Holmes to destruction. Moriarty is not only on a level with Holmes - he Is Holmes in reverse, an antichrist figure. He has the same perfectly logical mind, the same fondness for philosophy. In trying to put himself in the place of the villain to determine his next move, Holmes merely has to think about what he himself would do.

Inconsistencies: The reader is confronted with several inconsistencies in Watson's account. Why would Holmes take Watson with him in his flight? Save for companionship, there was no good reason to expose the two of them to such danger. Watson was certainly a dead give-away to the presence of Holmes. And how did Moriarty hire a special train so quickly? Why did it take three whole days to arrest the Moriarty gang? What made Holmes think Moriarty would be arrested in London when he clearly knew him to be on the Continent? Is the reader to ignore these questions on the supposition that Holmes seemed to have a premonition of his sacrificial fate?

Suspense: From the opening lines of the story, the reader is aware that Holmes will be killed; suspense mounts concerning the circumstances that will surround his death. From the moment that Watson leaves his friend at Reichenbach, Holmes' inevitable fate overtakes him like the turbulent waters which roar, inevitably ceaselessly below. The realization of the end of Holmes is, for the reader as for Watson, gradual yet inescapable.

Denouement: The sorrow of the reader is doubled because he must witness the grief of Watson: "It was the sight of that alpenstock which turned me cold and sick..." Holmes' last speech and Watson's closing remarks about the "best and wisest man" form another ideal Holmesian **epitaph**. (It sounds like a paraphrase of Plato's eulogy of Socrates.) The story had a perfect and appropriate ending in the form of Greek tragedy, but would be unacceptable to the public.

Doyle's Estimate: This story ranked fourth among Doyle's preferences. The exotic locations, the constant feeling of motion and suspense, the superb character studies of Holmes, Watson, and Moriarty definitely make it one of the best stories ever penned by Doyle. In the creation of Moriarty he added another masterful touch to the galaxy of characters to oppose Holmes. He is the perfect counterpart, an alter-ego. Even their defiant repartee is brilliantly matched. Somehow it softens the shock of Holmes' death to realize that he sacrificed his life to destroy a force that was as representative of evil as he was of good. (Consult character analysis at back.)

Reichenbach Falls: The selection of the site of Holmes' death was pure genius. Doyle had visited the place, been awed by it, and decided that it was a fitting tomb for the forces of good and evil, personified in Holmes and Moriarty. For this reason, Doyle spent considerable time on its description, producing some of the most powerful word pictures in the Canon. The "Sherlock Holmes footpath" trodden by Moriarty, Watson, and Holmes is still in existence, and plaques were erected to commemorate the Great Struggle and the stay of Watson and Holmes in Meiringen. There is a Sherlock Holmes Hotel and an Adler Hotel (no relation) in Meiringen. In 1968 the great Holmes-Moriarty Struggle was re-enacted before television cameras at the famous Falls.

Reaction: Doyle wrote just two words in his diary to record the consummation: "Killed Holmes!" Protest mail flooded in, one letter beginning: "You brute!" Readers were horrified and all of London was in a furor over such a dastardly deed on the part of Doyle. For nine years Doyle played deaf to entreaties; in the meantime, Holmes assumed the stature of a tragic hero who had valiantly laid down his life.

Second Thoughts: In 1902 Doyle produced another Holmesian adventure, but then deemed it prudent to date it prior to the Reichenbach tragedy. The Hound of the Baskervilles takes the form of a retrospection rather than a resurrection. But that came a year later. In 1903 Doyle succumbed to various pressures and retrieved the world's most famous detective from that "dreadful chasm" that he might continue to be the "world's foremost champion of justice" for another twenty-three years.

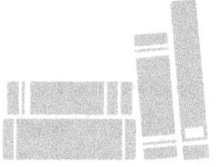

THE RETURN OF SHERLOCK HOLMES

"THE EMPTY HOUSE"

This story has probably engendered more commentary, criticism, and speculation than any other in the Canon. To explain a way out of that "dreadful chasm" for Holmes and account for three years of silence (remaining dead to the world and Watson as well) was bound to involve inconsistencies.

Discrepancies: The first inconsistency is that the Christian name of both Moriarty brothers (Professor and Colonel) was "James." Perhaps this was a mistake on Watson's part (certainly not on Holmes'). Or, as the noted Sherlockian, Vincent Starrett hypothesized, "one might well suppose some sort of sinister pattern..."

Holmes' treatment or neglect of poor Watson seems deceitful and cruel. Feigning death to trap the remaining members of the Moriarty gang seems incompatible with what Holmes said in Fina about all of them being arrested.

Does it not appear strange that Moran, the world-famous sharpshooter, should follow Moriarty and Holmes to the Falls, unarmed? Failing in his attempt to finish Holmes off by hurling stones, would he not have notified the gang when he returned to London that Holmes was safe and Moriarty dead?

Holmes' account of his hiatus (wanderings in the meantime) is hardly feasible considering the fact that many of the places he claims to have visited were in political upheaval at the time and a European would not have been welcome.

While fundamentalists accept the account with blind faith, some critics have used their imagination. Was Holmes the victim of amnesia after his traumatic ordeal? Did any of Moran's rocks strike the target? Was Holmes engaged in secret government service on the Continent? Did Mycroft neglect to notify Watson of their work? Or did love come at last to Holmes in the person of Irene Adler Norton?

Changes: Some commentators speculate that the resurrected Holmes was an imposter. They base their belief on the fact that the new man was not a cocaine user, that he had a more flippant attitude toward the law and criminals than ever before, especially obvious in his facetious jibing of Moran. Or, was there no comeback at all, the stories being a figment of lonesome Watson's imagination?

Watson: The poor medic seems to have suffered two bereavements in three years: his best friend and, apparently, his wife. Holmes (true or false) expresses sympathy and advises work as the best cure.

Antagonist: The challenge of this story is a fitting welcome home present for the Master and something to take Watson's mind off his sorrow. Col. Sebastian Moran, the "second most dangerous man" in London, is a worthy successor of Moriarty.

Anyone who can shoot a man through an open third-story window (British "second floor") from the street below is no mean adversary.

Trap: But Holmes prefers to use his head rather than his shooting skill (MUSG) to catch Moran. The wax bust is fitting bait for a big-game hunter of the past. Of course, Holmes was unduly optimistic when he said: "the bullets alone" were enough to convict Moran. The study of ballistics would not become part of police procedure until 1909, and it seems that without such evidence, Holmes was unable to achieve a conviction - at least not a death sentence because he refers in ILLU to Moran as living.

Comeback And Decline: Most critics tend to agree with the Cornish fisherman whom Doyle was fond of quoting: "When Mr. Holmes fell over that cliff, he may not have killed himself, but he was never quite the same man afterwards." The pre-Reichenbach stories are simple and more engaging.

However, absence made the hearts of Englishmen and Americans grow fonder. For American rights to this story, Doyle was paid $5,000, possibly the highest fee ever paid for a single short story at that time. Doyle continued to write stories until 1927, three years before his death.

The wax bust stratagem was also used in MAZA because that story was based on a play (*The Crown Diamond*) which, in part, was based on this very story.

Doyle credited his second wife, Jean, for the idea he used to explain Holmes' comeback.

"THE NORWOOD BUILDER"

High school anthologies with a Holmes story usually include SPEC or this one because they are both action-packed. The basic conflict in this case is between Holmes the wary and Inspector Lestrade the certain. Not Watson, but Lestrade functions as the foil to highlight the superiority of the sleuth. McFarlane makes a dramatic entrance, and curiosity is aroused about the identity of the guilty party and how he will be exposed.

Evidence: The evidence against a young attorney is much too obvious to delude Holmes who is skeptical about it. The reader is aware of the exact moment when the mystery is solved for Holmes: on finding a bloody fingerprint. Lestrade shouts, "That's final." And it is. Holmes' repetition of those very words assures the reader he knows the secret and that he and Lestrade have reached opposite conclusions from identical evidence.

Ruse: In a farcical scene, not unlike his ruse in SCAN, Holmes smokes the guilty architect out of hiding by sending billows of smoke into the secret compartment and having the constables shout, "Fire, fire!" As in CASE and MANW, victim and villain are the same person. The villain emerges the fool with Inspector Lestrade not much his inferior.

Characterization: The very title of the story might prepare the reader for the eventual outcome. The newspaper account, by mentioning the old man's eccentricities, foreshadows his bizarre scheme. Oldacre is a bit overdrawn as a character, one of the villainous villains in the Saga. His youthful sadism in turning loose a cat in an aviary (Similar sadism is portrayed by Brackenstall in ABBE.) warns his fiancee of his cruelty, and she wisely marries another man. Vindictively, Oldacre sends her a wedding gift of her portrait horribly mutilated. Motivation is made credible as he apparently nourished his desire for revenge through the years to strike at her through her only son. Given the warped mind of the man, the surprising part of the story is that it took him twenty-three years to pull such a stunt. Holmes often complains about the lack of originality in the criminal field. Mediocrity failed to stimulate him, especially after the demise of Moriarty.

Climax: Where does it occur? For Holmes, discovery of the fingerprint constituted the **climax**, but for the reader it is delayed until the fire leads to enlightenment. Doyle uses **irony** in the ruse of exposure: that Holmes should light a fire to uncover the man whose remains were supposedly destroyed by fire.

Police Procedures: The story is definitely dated in the lack of police procedures. No tests were made on the animal remains, and bloodstains were not tested to determine if they were human. It seems dubious that experienced constables and firemen would not detect the nature of the animal bones.

Fingerprints: Lestrade presented the fact that no thumbprints are alike as though it were a novel idea. Historically, England was discussing Galton's theory of the uniqueness of fingerprints. The story is dated 1895; one year later, fingerprints were first used in the detection of crime by Sir William Herschel in Bengal.

Legal Matters: Doyle's ignorance of or inattention to legal matters comes to the fore again (SCAN, FIVE) where there is a single witness instead of two. In this case that witness is the sole beneficiary of the will. To make the error more glaring, that character is himself a lawyer. This is another example of Doyle's neglect of details while he concentrated on achieving a dramatic effect.

Vocabulary: Freemason - a member of an extensive secret order or fraternity.

"THE DANCING MEN"

As in Five, Holmes reproaches himself for not being able to avert the tragedy of his client's death. In both cases his feeling of remorse incites his determination to see that justice is done.

Mind-Reading: Prior to the arrival of Cubitt, the client, Holmes engages in a mind-reading exercise on Watson. The latter's bewilderment turns to amused understanding when Holmes explains the chain of associations that led logically to his conclusion. A Holmesian aphorism is forthcoming: "Every problem becomes childish when once it is explained to you."

Check-Book: For some unknown reason, Watson's check-book is locked in Holmes' drawer. Was Watson in the habit of overdrawing? Are commentators correct in finding an explanation in a later remark that half his pension is spent at the racetrack (SHOS)?

Client: Hilton Cubitt like Grant Munro (YELL) married an American whose inexplicable behavior involved a secret. Cubitt is too much of a gentleman to force his wife's confidence because of a former promise and he is the unfortunate victim.

The Code: What at first appeared to Watson to be childish pranks are later described by him as a "grotesque frieze." The chalk drawings of dancing men are eventually interpreted by Holmes, but not in time to avoid bloodshed. He inspired reader and client with confidence by acknowledging that he had written a monograph in which he identified one hundred and sixty ciphers. The warning, "Elsie, prepare..." sounds like the prophet Amos, "Israel, prepare to meet thy God."

Modus Operandi: What escaped everyone's notice at the violent scene was quickly discovered by Holmes. His interrogation of the servants is further enlightening. Eventually, he baits the villain with his code and lures him into the trap.

The Code: The origin of the code used by Doyle has been ascribed to different sources. Gavin Brend's explanation carries more weight than the others. Apparently, Doyle saw the autograph of a seven-year-old boy in the dancing figures. The boy's father, proprietor of a hotel, was named Cubitt - the very name given the client in the story. Neither Cubitt nor Doyle laid claim to inventing the code.

Mistakes: Several mistakes were made when the code appeared in the *Strand Magazine* so that readers were unable to decipher the message properly. Eventually, mistakes were corrected.

Suspense: For sheer suspense, this well-told tale ranks with SPEC. In addition to the mysterious code which the reader feels challenged to work out, Doyle has Watson use one of his literary devices to foreshadow the ending. Watson apologizes at the outset for not being able to provide a happy ending. He gives a further turn to the screw by announcing that the horrible facts made Ridling Thorpe Manor a household word through the length and breadth of England.

Tension: One of Doyle's most masterful techniques for mounting tension is his use of dialogue. When the frantic pair arrive on the scene, the constables indicate they are too late. "Are you the detectives?" indicates something terrible has occurred, instilling fear. "Are you the surgeons?" suggests there is life, but it implies violence, which invokes horror. The final declarative statement, "If you save her it will probably be for the gallows," specifies that Mrs. Cubitt is still alive, but what has she done in her distraught state? The cumulative effect of this dialogue is matched only by the tragic folk ballad.

Conclusion: The **denouement** occurs slowly, but it is not anticlimactic. The reader is eager to meet the villain and understand his motivation. Like Killer Evans (3GAR), he is a disappointment because he is a typical Bret Harte American, a gangster from Chicago. He is another tough guy with a heart of gold who never intended the consequences of his actions.

Popularity: Understandably, Doyle placed this (third) on his list of favorites.

"THE SOLITARY CYCLIST"

This is one of those rare instances in the Canon where the story is less a tale of deduction than an adventure story. As in YELL and more obviously in VEIL, events and their outcome do not pivot around Holmes' investigation. He does arrive to tidy up loose ends and lend an air of authority. Still, he arrives (as in DANC) too late to prevent the inevitable outcome of circumstances.

Shortcomings: Holmes is out of character in not taking more immediate action. (See SILV where he admits a similar mistake.) His irascibility in upbraiding Watson so severely for his inept ways of gathering information provides a perfect opportunity for Watson to whisper "Norbury" (see YELL), but he fails to take advantage of it.

Fisticuffs: Holmes atones for his testiness with a delightful vein of humor as he narrates to Watson his encounter with Woodley. Holmes, of course, was an excellent boxer and singlestick player from his college days. He was also an expert in Japanese baritsu wrestling; villains did well to avoid encounters with him in which fisticuffs were involved (see ILLU).

The Marriage: This scene is melodramatic and rather absurd. Any clergyman, "unfrocked" or not, would realize that a forced marriage is invalid. Perhaps he was counting on great ignorance on the parts of those involved. Williamson was doubly guilty for ignoring this point of Church law and for attempting to solemnize a marriage after his deposition.

Title: The title is ambiguous. Just who Is the "solitary cyclist"? Evidently Carruthers is meant; but the client, Violet Smith, also rode and was the first to be met on a bike. Doyle might have changed the title to the plural as he did for REIG. (Note: the bicycle supposedly ridden by Miss Smith is still in existence - it was discovered by a Ralign manufacturer and placed on display at the 1951 Sherlock Holmes Exhibition.)

Syntax: Doyle uses sharp, effective prose to move the story. After a long descriptive passage of compound-complex sentences, he brings the reader up short with an effective brief simple sentence. Sometimes he uses a series of short sentences to build tension.

Dialogue: Doyle is superb with dialogue. Here he makes it terse, clipped, effective. When Holmes describes his fight, Doyle employs swift, staccato rhythm to reflect the action. At the **climax**, the exchange of words is marvelous:

You're too late. She's my wife.

No, she's your widow.

Invitation: Holmes' knowledge of boxing got Doyle an invitation in 1909 from the editor of the New York Morning Telegram to judge the heavyweight championship of the world. Doyle declined.

Vocabulary: menage - a household; the persons taken collectively (French).

surplice - a white garment worn over the clothes by the officiant at a religious service.

unfrocked - deprived of the powers and privileges of a clergyman.

public house - a combination hotel and tavern.

"THE PRIORY SCHOOL"

The most dramatic entrance ever made at 221B Baker Street occurs in this story and Watson writes it up in such a way as to emphasize the surprise and **irony** involved. The client enters, "the embodiment of self-possession....," and immediately proceeds to faint. When the huge figure, Dr. Huxtable, arises, he explains that ten-year-old Lord Saltire has been abducted from his preparatory school.

Snobbery: Holmes and Watson have been accused of social snobbery, an all too common vice in Victorian England. Watson described the adventure of Illu as "the high point of Holmes' career" because Edward VII was presumably involved. Watson seems shocked that a man of Sir Robert Norberton's station could commit murder in Shos; while Holmes considers the feelings of Lady Brackwell in CHAR more important than those of the maid, Agatha, whose heart he might break in the course of the investigation. In this story, Holmes seems to find the disappearance of a duke's son of greater import than the "Abergavenny murder."

Holmes: The Master's pretense of a sprained ankle lends comic relief to a case that threatens to add to the number of tragedies. A murder, the fear of scandal, the imposed secrecy, the frantic search, all heighten suspense. Holmes shows himself capable of writing another monograph - on bicycle tires, since he was familiar with "forty-two different impressions." His suspicions become hard facts and the Duke of Holderness is not spared the facts of his compromising position.

Inspiration: Doyle got his idea for one of his devices in this story from an article that had appeared in the Strand nine months before. Ancient horseshoes shaped to simulate cow tracks had been discovered and Doyle pressed into service this item from current events.

Tire Tracks: Doyle was taken to task for his theory, important in the story, that the hind tire of a bicycle bore the weight and thus indicated the direction in which the rider traveled. Experiments were made and the issue was debated with experts on both sides of the tracks.

The Duke: As a character, this man is one of the best vignettes in the entire Saga, much nobler than the Noble Bachelor. His duplicity warrants the treatment given him by Holmes who demands a reward for his services. Conjectures concerning his true identity led to the popular theory that he was the eighth Duke of Devonshire whose estate lay in Derbyshire. Near this estate is the town of Macclesfield which approximates Mackleton in the story.

His Sons: One is disappointed at never meeting the lad whose disappearance prompted the story. The clemency shown Wilder, the half-brother, is understandable.

Vocabulary: entail - a restricted line of succession or inheritance (noun).

"BLACK PETER"

What little use Doyle made of his experience as surgeon for harpooners aboard the whaler Hope in 1880 appears in this story. Holmes' methods never fail to intrigue Watson, especially when they bring his partner home from a butcher shop with a harpoon under his arm in time for breakfast. Holmes' firsthand experiment to transfix a pig with a single blow, and his newspaper ad which produces burly seamen inquiring for a Captain Basil, bewilder his friend who is above "forcing a confidence."

Inspector Hopkins: "Black Peter," an appellation referring to the victim's moods rather than his swarthy appearance, was found transfixed to the wall. Inspector Stanley Hopkins, who receives help in schoolboy fashion from the Expert, tries to impress his superior with the way he applied the Holmesian "Methods," but two and two never add up to four in this case for the aspiring detective. The cards are so stacked against him that by strong coincidence the initials of both the victim and the villain are identical.

Holmes: Annoyed by inept procedures, Holmes delights in rubbing salt into wounds with remarks like, "I understand from the inquest that there were some objects you failed to overlook." The Inspector dons the dunce's cap as the story progresses, always accepting what seems obvious as factual. Critics are as hard on Holmes as he was on Hopkins for spending three days to acquire information via telegraph that was accessible within hours had he used the telephone across the street.

Deduction: This is one of those stories Doyle might have had Holmes tell instead of Watson in order to focus on the art of deduction. Better though, Doyle makes Inspector Hopkins serve the same purpose - to allow Holmes to teach and demonstrate through trial and error. Where Watsonians might have cringed at such abuse, a Scotland Yard inspector is fair game. Hopkins impulsively jumps to the most likely conclusions without considering the possibility of alternatives. Under Holmes' prodding and sarcastic chidings, he painfully learns to employ the Cartesian "Methodical Doubt." At a later date (ABEE), Holmes gives Hopkins credit for recognizing an important case when one presents itself.

Watson's Dramatics: The subplot manages to complicate the story with red herrings - the better to instruct Hopkins. Watson is guilty of overindulging in rhetorical questions, the better to produce goose bumps as he awaits the return to the scene of the crime of the murderer. "What savage creature was it which might steal upon us out of darkness? Was it...would he...?"

Denouement: When John Neligan arrives, he proves to be an anticlimactic disappointment and a frustrating red herring. The ending contains the favorite devices of using an advertisement to trap the villain and a confession with a seafaring theme.

Vocabulary: Cartesian - pertaining to the doctrine or method of René Descartes, a French philosopher.

"CHARLES AUGUSTUS MILVERTON"

Without a doubt, this is the blackest of the ten blackmail stories in the Saga. No other story has for its title the name of the villain. The eponymous character (person for whom the story is named) is not only a professional blackmailer but, in Holmes' experience, the very "king of the trade."

Holmes' Contempt: Never before or after was Holmes so demonstrative in his disdain for an adversary. (With Moriarty there was a deep respect for the man's powers, fiendish as they were, and a sense of regret for their misuse.) So despicable and ruthless is Milverton that on meeting him, Holmes rejects his handshake and offers instead a countenance of granite. Watson makes much of Holmes' loathing and frustration in trying to come to terms with the likes of such a man, in order to justify the felonies they will commit in their effort to checkmate him.

Vicarious Experience: Unique to this case is the vicarious experience the two sleuths have as they sneak or race about in criminal shoes. Holmes seems to take a delight in finding himself in the position of lawbreaker; Watson rationalizes and soothes his conscience.

Engagement: Holmes' use of disguise to ferret information from Milverton's maid is rendered memorable by the fact that he becomes engaged to Agatha. At Watson's disedification, Holmes assures him that he has a rival ready to fill his shoes. One would think Agatha worthy of being the fifth person toasted at the annual Baker Street Irregulars' meeting in January after Holmes, Watson, Irene Adler, and Mrs. Hudson.

Partnership: The relationship between the incomparable pair makes this an interesting and amusing study. Juxta posed with the horrible scenes of suspense are the humorous incidents which almost serve as comic relief. The boyish Watson takes umbrage at being excluded from the case and threatens to inform (blackmail?) the police about Holmes' intended burglary. Holmes gives in, amused to think that after being roommates for years, they just might become cellmates.

Resisting Arrest: After breaking and entering, cracking a safe, witnessing a cold-blooded murder, destroying someone else's property, resisting arrest, they casually joke with Inspector Lestrade when he reads the only physical description of Watson to be found in the Canon. Knowing about Watson's bum leg, the Inspector would hardly suspect him to be the villain who ran at top speed and scaled a wall to escape.

Clemency: Proportionate to their nonchalance is Holmes' conviction that since certain crimes cannot be touched by law, they thereby justify public revenge. Critics have raised eyebrows over the ethical issues involved. But most readers have merely winked.

Contemporary Note: In an essay contest on the favorite villain in the Canon, the greatest number of entries dealt with "loathesome Milverton." One nominated Holmes himself on the basis of stories such as this. The winning entry dealt with Baron Gruner of ILLU.

"THE SIX NAPOLEONS"

Holmes scores another cerebral triumph in this unusual story, the facts of which strike the police and Watson as possibly a case of monomania, an idée fixe (French for obsession) with Napoleon the object of hatred. After four broken statues and one murder, Holmes detects a pattern. Once the Italian iconoclast is captured, the story resembles BLUE.

Understanding: In addition to his knowledge of human nature, the Master demonstrates a knowledge of human institutions, in this case, the Press. He proves that such knowledge is power.

Induction: This story is the rare instance where Holmes describes his reasoning process as Induction rather than Deduction. Since most of the time Holmes is reasoning from the particular to the general, perhaps he should have been saying "induction" all along.

Praise: When Holmes recapitulates the facts, explaining how he drew inferences, Inspector Lestrade pays him one of the highest compliments. Watson (faithful Boswell!) notes the effect on his partner and then puts him right back in character, providing a satisfactory, sentimental ending.

Mr. Hudson: The sculptor has given those who like to read into stories, and between lines, a springboard. Is he any relation to Holmes' housekeeper? Or to the blackmailer of Justice Trevor (GLOR)?

Motivation: In this adventure, motivation poses a big question. From unlikely beginnings comes a pattern that formed a mosaic. The title of the story ensures suspense because the reader knows how far the murderer-thief will go.

Minor Character: Horace Harker, the journalist who could not pull himself together in order to write the facts of his own story and rush in an eye-witness account, is one of the more interesting minor characters to lighten the pages of the Canon.

Allusion: Doyle uses an allusion in ABBE which almost belongs in this story about "Napoleons" when he has Holmes say that an unexpected turn-of-events is not his Waterloo but his Marengo. Just as the Battle of Marengo began in defeat but ended in victory, so an investigation beginning with defeats in the form of broken busts ends in the criminal's capture.

High Praise: Critics consider this one of the best-told tales by Doyle with lots of intrigue, suspense, another night vigil, and satisfaction at the end.

Vocabulary: monomania - a mental disorder in which a person, otherwise rational, is obsessed with one idea or subject.

Mafia - a secret criminal organization of Sicilians and Italians.

"THE THREE STUDENTS"

It hardly seems fitting to label this an "adventure" when it is a pure detective puzzle-story, similar to SILV. Holmes comes off comfortably well as a sleuth, but uncomfortably as a human being. When asked by Soames to help in an investigation, he shows annoyance at having his work interrupted. Sarcastically, he jibes at Watson and pays him a left-handed compliment when he perceives how dense Soames proves in the face of significant clues. Watson was well-versed in reading his friend's moods and understood that "without his scrapbooks, his chemicals and his homely untidiness, he was an uncomfortable man."

Setting: The setting has provoked good-natured controversy: Is the "great University town" Oxford or Cambridge? The decision is made no easier by Watson's resolve to avoid language that would limit the events to one place. The most popular bet is Oxford for several reasons: first, Holmes refers to a "quadrangle," a distinctly Oxonian term; second, Holmes seems familiar with the terrain, whereas in MISS he seems unfamiliar with Cambridge (Is this a sign that Holmes' own University was Oxford and not Cambridge? This is a favorite topic of discussion among Sherlockians of both schools); third, Oxford's Bodleian library would be the perfect place to conduct research on early English charters (another of his outside interests which included music, boxing, philology, and anthropology).

On the other hand, the playing fields of Cambridge were covered in a black clay as in this story. It is possible, of course, that Gilchrist was practicing at a non-University field outside the town, which would explain why Holmes had to walk five miles to reach it.

The Examination: Another element to be examined is the content of the examination. Soames is supposed to have selected half a chapter of Thucydides for translation. This is hardly a challenge, even "sight-unseen," because every Greek scholar would not only have read but also be thoroughly familiar with this famous historian. Also, the chapters of Thucydides are very short and could not take up three long sheets of printer's proofs. Such inconsistencies have led some commentators to theorize that the whole adventure was merely a hoax conceived by Watson and abetted by Soames to stimulate the despondent Holmes. Perhaps the clues and suspects were just a little too conveniently defined.

The "Least Likely": Doyle's use of the least likely person as criminal is a bit too convenient and hardly a challenge to Holmes' powers, but the idea would become a standard feature of the British mystery novel in the early twentieth century. Indeed, many writers still cling to the dry, outmoded "puzzle" approach. Doyle's use of the trick is very obvious: McLaren is suspected because of his unstable character and poor Daulat Ras, on the prejudicial grounds that he is a foreigner; only the noble Gilchrist of untarnished image is unsuspected, and he, of course, is the criminal. Doyle hesitated to make such a "perfect Englishman" a thorough villain and has Gilchrist redeem himself; but he makes up for this by making the butler a perfect gem. Motivation and exposure are the main points of interest, well handled by Doyle.

"THE GOLDEN PINCE-NEZ"

The stormy weather that presaged tragedy in FIVE characterizes the opening of this story, with similar results. It is not a client who arrives at the storm's height in this story, but Inspector Stanley Hopkins.

Hopkins: The young inspector seems to be a humble man, willing to learn and eager to capitalize on Holmes' abilities. Had he been otherwise, he would not have approached Holmes for help after the treatment he received in BLAC. He takes the Master's taunt with good nature.

Clues: The only positive clues are the dying man's words and a pair of golden pince-nez, important enough to entitle the story. They are second only to the famous black hat of BLUE for the number of deductions drawn from them by observant Holmes. More telling, perhaps, is a negative clue: absence of footprints leaving the home after the storm. What that tells Holmes, added to evidence gathered from his scattered cigarette ashes, leads to a most dramatic denouement.

Suicide: Professor Coram's wife is not thwarted in her suicide attempt as were Pinner in STOC and Amberley in RETI. She succeeds before Holmes can stop her. The woman's frenzy to recover her diary (an object that will undo Baron Gruner in ILLU) had resulted in accidental murder.

Holmes' Achievements: Finding Holmes engaged over a palimpsest, a document written upon twice, the original ordinarily in Latin, critics infer that he had a knowledge of Latin (in addition to German, Italian, and French). His acceptance of the French Legion of Honor (mentioned among another series of unchronicled cases and achievements) is noteworthy in view of the fact that he declined the English knighthood (3GAR).

Watson: Doyle uses Watson to reflect Holmes' growing interest in the case. Of course, Watson was misled: "I had never known him handle a case in such a half-hearted fashion." Later he employs typical Watsonian **metaphor** to describe his partner. The reader and Watson know that Holmes knows something of vital importance. Ordinarily, Doyle makes Holmes his mouthpiece to philosophize on Nature, but at the opening of this story, it is Watson he uses.

The Professor: The character of the professor is more repugnant in Doyle's dramatic presentation than in his wife's confession-account. His hypocritical "God bless you, Anna" each time that she withholds information about his conduct makes him an interesting specimen of religious pietism.

Vocabulary: spirit-lamp - a lamp operated by the burning of alcohol, probably used to heat Holmes' coffee.

Nihilist - a member of a revolutionary movement in Russia in the 19th century, believing that reform was possible only in the overthrow of political, economic, and social institutions.

"THE MISSING THREE-QUARTER"

In fifteen crimeless cases, this is the only one where Holmes' presence constitutes a rude intrusion. That his methods are of prime importance argues well for the inclusion of this story in the Canon. His sleuthing just as validly uncovered the fact that no crime had been committed.

The Client: Cyril Overton is one of the most likable of the Holmesian clients. His assumption that everyone knew Rugby Football and the big game between Cambridge and Oxford adds humor when he finds so knowledgeable a man as Holmes so ignorant of athletic heroes.

Messages: First comes the enigmatic message from Overton who assumes Holmes will understand his terms. Scrutinizing a blotter to learn the content of a telegram, Holmes realizes the matter is serious. Cleverly obtaining (illegally) a copy of the telegram from the telegraph office (claiming there were at least seven ways of getting such information!), he picks up a scent. (Holmes frequently uses the mystical number seven in his boasts - see COPP and NAVA.)

Best Friend: Holmes resorts not to his best friend, Watson, but to man's best friend - the dog. Pompey takes him where he wants to go, but Holmes is definitely an intruder at the deathbed scene of the missing athlete's wife. Dr. Leslie Armstrong, his adversary so far, seems a little too willing to let bygones be bygones; perhaps Holmes' promise of secrecy is all it takes to placate the man.

Drugs: Watson indicates at the beginning of this story that he feared his friend would return to drugs as a compensation for boredom. This case occupies his mind and energy and never again is cocaine mentioned. Many feel Holmes found other interests and, always being in control, simply decided to occupy himself with them, no longer craving stimulation.

Characterization: Doyle does a good job with lightning strokes to depict three characters. There is Dr. Armstrong who is so provoked by Holmes' interference that he appears villainous; Lord Mount-James, an old Scrooge; and the young, giant Overton. Like CASE, MANW, and other stories, this tale raises questions in the reader's mind about "the morning after." The simple ending is quiet, evocative, and fitting: "We passed from that house of grief into the pale sunlight of the winter day."

Vocabulary: sixteen stone - a variable measure of weight. In England, fourteen pounds avoirdupois (approximately 225 pounds).

loose-box - in a stable the enclosure where a horse is left loose or unhaltered.

three-quarter - a player in Rugby Football whose regular position is between the halfback and the fullback.

"THE ABBEY GRANGE"

This case begins with the scene that best typifies the spirit of the Holmes adventures and contains one of the most oft-quoted lines in the Canon. Holmes awakens Watson near dawn on a wintry morning to join him in an adventure with the vivacious: "Come, Watson, come! The game is afoot!" Watson rises eagerly; surely there is no greater sign of friendship! Shakespeare used "the game is afoot" in both I Henry IV and Henry V.

Compassion: This is another case where Holmes shows himself to be a champion of a higher law rather than an unbending proponent of British law. As with Turner (BOSC), Ryder (BLUE), Wilder (PRIO), and Dr. Sterndale (LION), Holmes follows his own conscience, setting himself up as a judge. He literally constitutes Watson the jury. Watson, emulating the Master's compassion, acquits Crocker.

Secrecy: Holmes feels no guilt in not revealing the murderer to the police; he has given them several clues as to the culprit's true identity and refuses to do more unless the blame falls on an innocent victim. (Holmes first makes sure that the Randall gang has a clear-cut alibi so that they will not be accused.) How does it happen, then, that Watson feels free to publish the case which would not only incriminate Crocker but show Holmes to be an accessory? Apparently, both Lady Brackenstall and her lover were dead by the time the story was published and were beyond the reach of the law.

Mouthpiece: Doyle very obviously uses Lady Brackenstall as a mouthpiece for his own views on the divorce law in England. He was president of the Divorce Law Reform Union and author of a famous tract upon the subject, which brought about the creation of a Royal Commission of Inquiry into the matter. (Doyle also uses Sterndale for the same purpose in DEVI.) Several other authors were also calling attention to the need for reform, notably George Bernard Shaw in his prefaces and plays (such as *Getting Married*).

Plot: The plot is well planned to create suspense and tie loose ends together. The opening paragraph keeps the reader guessing as to the nature of the exciting adventure; and Holmes' supposed decision to leave the case in the hands of the police keeps the reader wondering whether Holmes will have a change of heart.

Literature: Doyle shows Holmes to be better acquainted with literature than Watson gave him credit for at first. In this single story, Doyle puts two quotations on the lips of the Master; one from Shakespeare and one from Alcuin: "Vox populi, vox Dei" - "the voice of the people is the voice of God." Elsewhere, he cites the Bible (CROO, DANC, ILUU, 3GAB, RETI); Tacitus and Flaubert (REDH); Hafiz (CASE, and he alludes to Blazac and Horace); Baxter or Bradford or Neri (BOSC, and he alludes to Meredith); Horace (Blue); Shakespeare (EMPT and REDC in which he slightly misquotes the same line, 3STU); Keats (3GAB). Doyle often closes stories with an appropriate quotation, often foreign and often showing Holmes to be a classical scholar.

"THE SECOND STAIN"

Now that Holmes is retired, "notoriety" has become distasteful to him, and Watson has to furnish good arguments before Holmes will acquiesce to having any more of his cases published: Watson reasons that this important international case should culminate the entire series. Although Holmes plays for higher odds in this story than in most, the adventure is hardly "the crowning glory of (Holmes') career" in terms of deduction. It is a tribute to his patriotism that he describes it thus.

Watson: Perhaps Watson was especially taken with this case because he himself played an important part, his hunch proving to be correct. He suggests to Holmes that the murder of Lucas may be unconnected with the theft of the precious document, but Holmes dismisses the idea summarily. Yet, as it turns out, Watson was right, and Holmes was guilty of violating one of his favorite axioms which appears in this very story: "It is a capital mistake to theorize in advance of the facts."

Identities: It is difficult to deduce the real identities of "Trelawney Hope," "Lord Bellinger," and the potentate who wrote the all-important letter because Watson warns that he must be circumspect with details because of political restrictions. Watson, as usual, seems unduly taken with Lady Hilda Trelawney Hope's feminine charms; yet certainly few women have behaved as foolishly in jeopardizing their husbands' careers as she did.

Favorites: Doyle liked the story and placed it eighth on his list of favorites. It does have adventure and high suspense but, as a story of deduction, shows Holmes in poor form and relies upon heavy-handed coincidence for the main plot elements: Lucas is conveniently killed after the theft of the paper by a murderer whose mission was unconnected with the theft, thereby preventing Lucas from selling the document and giving Holmes time to recover it. Even so, Holmes might never have found its hiding place were it not for the coincidental misplacement of the rug over the secret compartment. The plot is full of contrivance but Doyle makes it more believable by having Holmes point out the very heavy-handedness of the coincidences to Watson.

Chronicled: Although Doyle includes mention of many unchronicled cases in his stories, this is the only one mentioned in an earlier story that he later decided to write about. In NAVA he alludes to the "adventure of the second stain," but here he fails to conform the actual story to its description in NAVA. NAVA's "Second Stain" has an autumn setting but this one takes place in July. The interview between Holmes and Monsieur Dubuque of the Paris police does not appear in this story. It also falls far short of the extravagant praise lavished on it by Watson in NAVA. In this "Second Stain" Holmes' "analytical methods" play an almost nonexistent role.

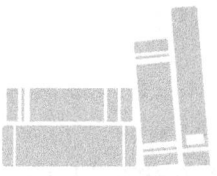

HIS LAST BOW

"WISTERIA LODGE"

The next best thing to having information is knowing where to obtain it and Holmes has found on many occasions that "There are no better instruments than discharged servants with a grievance." As in PRIO, Holmes worms inside information out of an ex-employee.

Inspectors: Not for the first time, Inspectors (Gregson and Baynes, this time) barge into 221B Baker Street in the middle of a consultation to arrest Holmes' client. (Recall their treatment of McFarlane in NORW.) Baynes temporarily impresses Holmes who compliments him on his attention to detail. His compliments soon alternate with warnings and eventually, the latter are more deserved. Baynes proved right for the wrong reasons when he guessed a woman was at the bottom of such weird happenings as an unusual invitation, a puzzling note, the disappearance overnight of an entire household, and a murder.

Watson: Watson has been given much undeserved credit for the so-called Holmesian deductions he made on meeting client, Eccles. The plotters had a method in their choice, and it was not the Holmesian method. Watson, the typical man in the street for all his work with Holmes, reacts in perfect accord with their plans when he sees Eccles as "conventional to the last degree." Eccles was used precisely because he would give that impression and provide someone with an alibi. That person, Garcia, needed a coffin instead.

Reluctance: Once again Watson goes against his better judgment to comply with that "ice-cold reasoning" of Holmes which made it impossible to shrink from any adventure. He had similar misgivings in MANW. As usual, however, Watson has no regrets in the end for accompanying his partner, although in CHAR, he must have had some uneasy moments.

Lack Of Interest: Perhaps the very reason that Eccles was chosen by the plotters as a stooge accounts for the lack of interest generated in the reader by his predicament. He is absolutely devoid of interest. True, Doyle loads the dialogue with adjectives like grotesque, strange, incredible, singular, unpleasant, and tragic. But it would seem the author doth protest too much. The end result is not curiosity as much as anti-climax, reflected in Doyle's original title: "The Singular Experience of Mr. John Scott Eccles."

Use Of Foil: The main note of interest lies in waiting for the embarrassment of Inspector Baynes, an aspect on which Doyle capitalized by building him up momentarily through praise from Holmes. Clever too, is the use of the newspaper to make both the criminals and Holmes think the inspector is on the wrong track. Holmes abused the newspaper himself in SIXN and ILLU.

Vocabulary: tete-a-tete - confidential; a private chat (French).

quarter-days - any of the days of the year when quarterly payments are due. In England, Lady Day

(March 25); Midsummer Day (June 24); Michaelmas (September 29); and Christmas.

"THE CARDBOARD BOX"

In an earlier adventure (NOBL) Holmes told Watson what this case bears out: jealousy transforms character. The contents of the infamous cardboard box are taken as a practical joke of medical students until Holmes is brought into the case, and then it is earmarked for detection.

Initials: Initially, we are back in the area of heavy coincidence. In BLAC, the initials of victim and villain were identical, which confused Inspector Hopkins. Here, the murderer sends a parcel in retaliation to the wrong sister - both have the same first initial.

Music: Whenever the perversity of human nature or the heavy hand of Fate oppresses Holmes (see BOSC), he takes refuge in music (FIVE). During their supper at a restaurant, he confides to Watson that he purchased for next to nothing a priceless violin that once belonged to Stradivarius. He speaks throughout the meal of Paganini.

Monographs: Holmes has occasion to use his uncanny knowledge, this time on the human ear. He claims to have written two monographs on the subject, which accounts for his speedy recognition.

The Strand: Doyle seems to have inspired the Strand editors to feature an article on the human ear with pictures of the ears of famous persons like Mozart, Newman, Dickens, and Dr. Oliver Wendell Holmes of whom Doyle said, "Never have I so known and loved a man whom I had never seen."

"THE RED CIRCLE"

Another importunate woman forces Holmes and Watson to listen to her plight (similar to Violet Smith in SOLI). Weird behavior on the part of a mysterious lodger sends the immortal pair on a spying expedition. Observance of smoking habits and scrutiny of notes furnish other tidbits, but Holmes never scorns trifles.

Agony Column: Holmes' reading habits lead him to important information in the agony column. His knowledge of Italian (hinted at in BOSC where he carried a pocket edition of Petrarch) enables him to decipher a message.

Inconsistencies: Oddly enough, instead of the language barrier serving a useful purpose for the fearful, the Italians use English in the agony column. (See ENGI where Germans spoke English at a period of crisis.) They also use the English alphabet to spell out their Italian words in code, it seems. The Italian alphabet contains no "K"; therefore, the message in real Italian would have made Holmes count to a "K" where an "L" was meant, etc. The message would then have read "Assemsa oeqicnkn" instead of "Attenta, pericolo." It was certainly foolhardy to remind the woman of their code by publishing it. Coincidence is also heavy-handed when everyone appears for the grand finale: Holmes, Watson, police, and lodger. At least it gives Holmes a good audience for the recapitulation. The last question is: Why wasn't all the information published in the agony column rather than using candles to draw attention?

Vocabulary: Carbonari - A nineteenth century secret society, organized in Italy to establish a republic.

"THE BRUCE-PARTINGTON PLANS"

This highly complex and detailed story of high intrigue similar to NAVA and SECO is all the more remarkable for containing the third and final appearance of Sherlock's brother Mycroft (after GREE and FINA) in the Canon.

Holmes: The drabness and monotony of the everyday world has plunged Holmes into depression, complaining of the lack of originality in the criminal world and expressing once again (see CHAR) what may be a sublimated yearning for a criminal career. (Later he will take delight in burglarizing Oberstein's house, also as in CHAR.) To take his mind from boredom he is writing a monograph on the Polyphonic Motets (medieval works written solely for voices) of (Orlando) Lassus. It would take a first-rate musician to be able to read such scores.

Mycroft: Holmes' older brother's second appearance at the Baker Street sitting rooms is such a departure from his normal routine that Holmes likens it to a "planet leaving its orbit." His presence is not vital to any of the stories in which he appears, yet his character is so unique as to enliven them greatly. In this tale Sherlock confides more about the nature of his brother's work to Watson - he not only works under the British Government, but "occasionally he is the British Government" - a veritable human storehouse of political facts and secrets.

Inconsistencies: Puzzling details keep this from being the story it might have been: for example, the incomprehensible and inane security measures and the handling of keys at the Woolwich Arsenal. Another is that so experienced a spy as Oberstein would leave some of his papers behind to furnish a clue for Holmes. That the villain would be spared capital punishment after committing cold-blooded murder and treason also raises questions. Why only a fifteen-year prison term?

Assets: Despite a plot full of inaccuracies and inconsistencies, Doyle produces good examples of his strong writing qualities. He had no eye for factual details - something that is especially obvious in light of his careless dating of cases, which has caused difficulties for hundreds of would-be Sherlockian chronologists. The plot is slowed by a dearth of retrospections but is appropriately mysterious, and Doyle's characterization is superb when Sherlock explains Mycroft's life style to Watson. He is also at his best using physical descriptions to reflect the characters' inner personalities, as in the cases of Mycroft, Johnson, and even Holmes himself. Atmospheric description is excellent at Caulfield Gardens and good dialogue in the many interviews throughout the story hasten the plot.

"THE DYING DETECTIVE"

A thoroughly suspenseful (albeit non-mystery) tale, DYIN has probably alarmed every devoted reader of Holmes. Of course, Holmes cannot die, but his malingering performance is so convincing, and Watson's fear so genuine, that the reader momentarily forgets the immortality of Holmes and worries along with Watson for the Master's life.

Watson: Watson is portrayed at his faithful best, eliciting sympathy as he is torn between respect for Holmes' wishes and concern for his health. With Watson, the reader witnesses the degeneration of Holmes.

Dramatics: Unfortunately, the story reveals an unpleasantly cold-blooded love of the dramatic in Holmes whose deception of poor Watson is difficult to understand. His excuse was that it was necessary to convince Watson of his illness in order that Culverton Smith be deceived. Holmes felt that Watson had talents, but among them, dissimulation found no place. (This was proven true when Watson attempted to deceive Gruner [ILLU] and failed.) Thus, Holmes thought it necessary to deceive Watson at times as in HOUN, DISA, and worst of all, Fina, having played dead for three years without informing Watson of the truth. It does seem that Holmes places his professional duties first, above personal loyalties. While readers expect this of him, nevertheless, his dramatic tendencies sometimes border on the inhuman side.

Suspense: Doyle maintains the major element of suspense in several ways. First, he establishes a gloomy atmosphere. Secondly, Doyle makes Holmes' degeneration gradual, with each step slightly more severe than the previous one. The physical frailty is followed by a weakening of the mind, and that by his complete loss of dignity and honor before Culverton Smith. Finally, Doyle maintains suspense through a "time-bomb" element - Holmes keeps Watson (and the reader) locked in the room for two hours as his sickness gets worse and worse; this raises a sense of helplessness which builds suspense.

Characters: The opening paragraphs give us one of the clearest thumbnail sketches of Holmes' eccentricities and, especially, his relationship with his landlady Mrs. Hudson, a too-little-explored character in the Canon. Culverton Smith is another fascinating creation, an odious villain. Not content with killing Holmes, he must come to the deathbed to gloat over the dying man; it is this greed for greater revenge that proves his undoing. Doyle realized the threat of the quiet villain (Moriarty,

FINA; Milverton, CHAR; Kemp, GREE, etc.), finding that quiet self-assurance can often be more frightening than the blustering of a tough person whose "bark is worse than his bite."

"THE DISAPPEARANCE OF LADY FRANCES CARFAX"

Of the ten cases based on someone's disappearance, this is the only one to indicate its nature and identify the person in the title. Watson might have named them The Disappearance Of: Hosmer Angel (CASE); Hatty Doran (NOBL); Godfrey Emsworth (BLAN); Jonas Oldacre (NORW); Lord Saltire (PRIO); Mrs. Josiah Amberley (RETI); Godfrey Staunton (MISS). SILV might have been prefaced with The Disappearance Of. Of course, none of these would have been an improvement on Watson's actual choice.

The Catalyst: Here as in PRIO, one never meets the catalyst. Her characterization is achieved only by what others say of her. Holmes sums up her type as "a stray chicken in a world of foxes" since she was a drifting and friendless spinster.

Watson: Watson would have done well to paraphrase the Master's word choice, substituting "invariably, she is the inciter of crime" for "she is the inevitable inciter of crime in others."

Watson's performance as Holmes' understudy may leave something to be desired, but does not deserve Holmes' illogical chiding. Watson had picked up Lady Frances' trail, discovering when and with whom she had left for London - a fact which Holmes disregards by leaving London and going to Montpelier unnecessarily disguised.

Superman: Doyle makes Holmes' uncommonly common arrival-in-the-nick-of-time resemble a Clark Kent transformation into Superman. Even Watsonians might prefer an occasional black eye than that he be rescued so incredibly.

Gothicism: At its height, Gothicism only threatened a person coming to his senses buried alive. The possibility of a woman's awakening in a coffin with another corpse is the ultimate of the macabre.

Writing: Doyle's writing is definitely superior to the content of this story. Good lines are given to Holmes and Watson. The Master explains: "On general principles it is best that I should not leave the country. Scotland Yard feels lonely without me, and it causes an unhealthy excitement among the criminal classes." Watson listens patiently to Holmes and later utters a typical understatement: "I was relieved at this sudden descent from the general to the particular."

Vocabulary: ouvrier - worker (French).

cabaret - restaurant, cafe, or tavern (French).

"THE DEVIL'S FOOT"

Watson wrote this tale at one of the rare suggestions of Holmes himself. (Holmes' usual attitude towards Watson's "romances" was one of disdain.) This promises a bizarre feature, and there is no disappointment.

Overwork: Again, as in REIG, Holmes' mental powers have driven his physical powers past their limit. It is the knowledge that even Holmes must occasionally submit to a doctor's warning to rest after overwork that makes him more reachable and charming to the reader. Watson also records that Holmes' collapse was partly due to occasional "indiscretions" of his own (cocaine, perhaps? Watson tells us in MISS that "the fiend was not dead but sleeping," yet here it seems that Holmes was not a victim of that boredom which previously drove him to the drug). Yet even on a vacation in solitary Cornwall, Holmes runs head long into his "strangest case."

Tobacco: Holmes displays an ambiguous attitude towards tobacco. The archetypal Victorian bachelor, Holmes apparently recognized and admitted his shortcomings, while ignoring the possibility of change. Mr. John L. Hicks tabulated thirty-odd stories in which Holmes smoked a pipe; in many others he added cigarettes (especially important in GOLD) and/or cigars.

The Drug: Holmes drastically underestimated the effects of the drug; and his experimentation with it leads to one of the best displays of mutual friendship between Holmes and Watson in the Canon. Watson saves the more sensitive Holmes from the drug's effects by literally moving him; and in return, Holmes offers a sincere apology for endangering Watson which gives another insight into "the great heart behind a great brain" that Watson relished all the more for its rare expression (see 3GAR).

Mood: Doyle ranked this ninth on his list of favorites, not without reason. It is one of the few tales in which mood rather than mystery or deduction takes priority and it contains some of the loveliest descriptive language in the Canon. The brooding landscapes of sensuous, lonely Cornwall establish a mood of sinister unseen evil. The inhuman and diabolical are likewise emphasized in the story, not only in the "unseen force" which kills Brenda and Mortimer Tregennis, but also in the many references to the devil throughout the story: diabolical, devil-ridden, monstrous. Sterndale calls Holmes "the devil Himself"; even the drug is called "Devil's Foot." The description of the drug's effects on Watson and Holmes is vivid! (No real drug produces effects like those of "Devil's foot root.")

Characters: Sharply emphasized here is Holmes' dual nature (energetic bloodhound vs. lethargic philosopher) and the amazing power of conscious mental detachment which enables him to concentrate upon a violin solo while in the midst of a London investigation or study neolithic rock-dwellings during a Cornwall case. Doyle uses Leon Sterndale as a mouthpiece for his views on divorce reform (see ABBE).

"HIS LAST BOW"

In the entire Canon, only two stories are narrated in the third person - this one and MAZA. In THOR, Watson admitted that in some cases he was either not present or played so small a part that they could only be told as by a third party. In this tale, Watson is not present for much of it.

Spy: It seems fitting that nothing short of a world war could withdraw Holmes from the solitary bee-keeping retirement on the Sussex Downs of which he had long dreamt; yet he responds to the summons with characteristic vigor and patriotism. Holmes' infiltration of the spy Von Bork's service through years of work must surely stand by the destruction of Moriarty as "the culminating event" in his career.

Alias: Holmes assumes the name "Altamont" (another creator/creation link: Altamont was Doyle's father's middle name) and appears as a "tall gaunt man of sixty." (It is generally agreed that the year of his birth was 1854 - see notes on GLOR - so this would be correct.) Watson is "a heavily built, elderly man with a gray moustache" (already noted in a police description in CHAR). Holmes finds him "the same blithe boy as ever" in spirit, characteristically joining the British with his "old service" - perhaps as a hospital volunteer.

That August: "The most terrible August" alluded to is that of 1914. Here is one case where the date poses no problem despite Watson's notorious inaccuracy. Von Bork called that time "England's week of destiny" - the week in which Russia invaded Germany, Germany invaded France, and England declared war on Germany.

Perception: Holmes was sensitive to the peril of that hour. He expresses the fear that "a good many of us may wither" before the winds of war, that this may be the last quiet talk he and Watson will enjoy. Trevor Hall suggests that Holmes was contemplating suicide due to oncoming blindness as a result of tobacco amblyopia. This is far from the Holmes who counseled Eugenia Ronder (VEIL) that her life was not her own: "Keep your hands off it." More widely accepted is the possibility that Watson died in the war, for many of the post-war stories in the Casebook do not sound like authentic Watson.

Housekeeper And Books: Was the "Martha" who here aids Holmes, Mrs. Hudson? There is nothing but romanticism to support this view. And why was Holmes' magnum opus, The Practical Handbook of Bee Culture (as well as the monumental work which he promised in ABBE, "a textbook which shall focus the whole art of detection into one volume") never published?

Title: This case presents another interesting titular history. Originally subtitled "The War Service of Sherlock Holmes" (inspired by General Humbert's inquiry as to whether Holmes was serving in WW I), it became "An Epilogue of Sherlock Holmes" in collections. This, plus the sentimental tone, suggests that once again Doyle was trying gracefully to have Holmes bow out. It was not to be, however, as Doyle should have known from his earlier attempt in FINA; and this tale which is the fitting conclusion to the Canon was to be succeeded by the stories which comprise the Casebook, published over a period of years from 1924-1927.

Finale: No other tale is quite so sentimental in depicting the sterling figures of a long friendship. Holmes' and Watson's unerring sense of justice and honor (counterbalancing Von Herling's statement that "honor is a medieval conception") and their enduring friendship make the pair "the one fixed point in a changing age." The permanence of absolutes is strongly affirmed in this story where they face an uncertain future with the Victorian steadfastness so typical of their creator.

Vocabulary: "window-breaking Furies" - Doyle's cynical description of suffragettes.

John Bull - a designation of the English people.

boodle - goods fraudulently obtained.

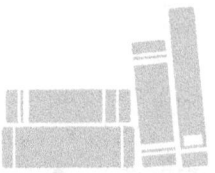

THE CASEBOOK OF SHERLOCK HOLMES

"THE ILLUSTRIOUS CLIENT"

For a story that opens in the relaxed atmosphere of a Turkish bath, it certainly changes its pace dramatically. Watson bears witness to the devotion and loyalty of his friendship at several points. First, he appreciates the fact that at the bath, he finds his friend more human and less reticent than anywhere else. Later he admits, however, that close as their friendship is, there is always an unbreachable gap to which he is resigned. His anxiety and concern over the murderous attack on Holmes requires reassurance from the Master himself that his condition is not as bad as the newspaper made out or as the bandages indicate.

Special Assignment: Watson is willing to do anything to assist his wounded friend. He is assigned an intensive, twenty-four-hour study of Chinese pottery. Poor Watson has his bluff called by the villain, Gruner, and never uses one piece of the information he crammed into his head, confirming Holmes' earlier observation (DYIN) that dissimulation was not among Watson's talents.

Baron Gruner: This diabolical Don Juan ranks among the outstanding villains in the Canon. Sir James Damery asserts:

"There is no more dangerous man in Europe." At the hands of his thugs, Holmes takes the beating of his life. Few blackguards, however, meet such poetic justice. He loses his diary to Holmes who turns it over to his fiancee, Violet de Merville, and he loses his sight and handsome face as the result of an ex-lover's revengeful acid throwing.

Holmes: Holmes is hard put to thwart this ruthless man's evil intentions. He uses every resort possible. First, he deals directly with Gruner, then he has a heart-to-heart talk with Violet. Here is the father-figure, the involved counselor. Holmes shrank from disillusioning Mary Sutherland in CASE, but he must send Violet the horrible diary to prevent the impending marriage.

The Client: Holmes is reluctant to accept this case when he realizes that he would be dealing with mystery at both ends. Sir James Damery is representing an "illustrious client." His name never passes between Holmes and Watson, but the story ends with Watson's enlightenment and Holmes' wink. Obviously, Edward VII is the "illustrious client," but Holmes had already dealt with Pope Leo XIII (BLAC), the King of Bohemia (SCAN), and had a tie pin from Queen Victoria (BRUC).

The Writing: Nowhere are the dialogue and description better. Doyle takes even the trite "Opposites attract" and rephrases it: "Extremes call to each other." Insight into Violet's character is displayed: "Violet showed abject filial obedience in secondary things to atone for her flagrant breach of it in her engagement."

Melodrama: It is true that the **episodes** are high melodramatic and sensational. The acid-throwing scene is gruesomely described by Watson who is in attendance.

Doyle's Own Estimate: Doyle was not especially proud of this plot, but he did not hesitate to say he would include the story among the best six he had written.

Vocabulary: doss-house - British slang: a cheap boarding house.

fence - slang: a dealer in stolen goods.

erysipelas - an acute infectious disease of the skin, accompanied by inflammation, chills, and fever.

carafe - a glass water jar; a decanter.

"THE BLANCHED SOLDIER"

This is the first tale (the other is DEVI) narrated by Holmes himself, and it must surely have been gratifying for Watson to read it. Holmes, to preserve the surprise ending, conceals many facts in his possession from the reader - something Watson would never do.

Watson: Holmes takes advantage of his position to have fun at his comrade's expense. Even his praise is characteristically unflattering as he calls Watson: "A confederate...to whom each development comes as a perpetual surprise..."

Narrator: Doyle must have labored to produce such a stiff, stilted style, leaving off the polished ending that is so characteristic of Watson. Using Holmes as narrator does make for variety, of course; if the public was not looking for it, perhaps the author was.

Ending: Doyle contrived a happy ending in having Godfrey Emsworth not a leper, as feared, but a victim of a milder skin disease. Earlier tales never catered to the public taste in this manner (FIVE, DANC, GREE).

Deduction: The Holmes/Dodd interview is reminiscent of a conversation Doyle once overheard between Dr. Joseph Bell and a patient: "Well, my man, you've served in the army?... Not long discharged?... A Highland regiment?... A non-com officer?... Stationed at Barbados?... You see, gentlemen, the man was a respectful man but did not remove his hat. They do not in the army, but he should have learned civilian ways had he been long discharged. He has an air of authority and is obviously Scottish. As to Barbados, his complaint is elephantiasis, which is West Indian and not British."

"THE MAZARIN STONE"

Like HISL, this story is narrated in the third person because Watson is not always present to see the action, nor is Holmes to inform him about it. Parts of the story - such as the conversation between Sylvius and Merton - are overheard by no one.

Inconsistencies: The details given of 221B do not coincide with previous accounts, e.g., the alcove, the bow window, the doors leading from the sitting room. Holmes appears extremely facetious, and his banter with Count Sylvius verges on inanity. (He begins to sound more like the talkative Lord Peter Wimsey than level-headed Holmes.) The scenes between Holmes and Sylvius seem forced and unnatural; only when Watson is on the scene does the story ring true, leading many commentators to believe that someone other than

Watson wrote the story and the scenes with Watson are the best because they were taken from notes of Watson's actual experience. It also seems highly unlikely that two thieves clever enough to steal one of the Crown Jewels would be so foolish as to discuss the robbery and bring the precious stone out into the open, in the apartment of London's greatest detective. But great as he was, would Holmes have risked life and limb in an unnecessarily dramatic ruse to eavesdrop on two men who would have killed him on the spot?

Critics: James Montgomery does not hesitate to label this story the "ugly duckling" of the saga. While not so literary in their verdicts, most critics are of the same mind. Doyle was not up to his usual level of performance in this case. Characterization borders on caricature and the stilted style is unlike the third person style of HISL, which is flowing and perceptive. Doyle is best when viewing Holmes' world through Watson's clouded eyes, romantic ideals, and honest pen.

Play: The reason for the story's shortcomings is that it is literally a play transferred to prose. It is based on *The Crown Diamond: An Evening with Sherlock Holmes,* a play which had an undistinguished run in London in 1921. In it, Doyle joined several Holmes stories into one. The villain was Colonel Sebastian Moran of EMPT fame; he became Count Sylvius in the story but retained the big-game hunting interests and the air-gun of Moran. (Note also the waxen-dummy ruse, similar to that of EMPT.) The action takes places in one "set," Baker Street; the opening description of the "familiar rooms" reads almost like a set description. Much of the story is conveyed, like a play, in dialogue. In trying to combine the best aspects of Holmes into one adventure - a device which might be successful in dramatic form but fails miserably in writing - Doyle attempted too great a task.

Sherlockismus: Doyle puts a clever self-evaluation on the lips of Holmes: "I am a brain... The rest of me is a mere appendix." It may be a hyperbole but it is a good Sherlockismus reminiscent of Descartes: "I think, therefore I am."

"THE THREE GABLES"

While his character may not be particularly noteworthy, the entrance of Steve Dixie at 221B is and warrants special mention by Watson. The latter claims it is one of the most dramatic he ever witnessed; only likening it to the entrance of a wild bull would do justice to the performance. (Clearly, it is second in interest only to that of the huge Huxtable in PRIO.) The boxer bursts into the room like a bull and then attempts to use bully tactics on Holmes who rides him in the manner of a picador. Holmes handles the case well because he knows how to handle people.

Holmesian Gestures: Two of his mannerisms may be noted in this story. The first is his habit of expressing surprise with a quick whistle (see RESI and SIX). The second is his way of persuading reluctant people to grant him an audience. Here he scribbles a question on a piece of paper and both the reader and the recipient wonder what is to come. Holmes has the keenness in each of his five senses that is usually possessed only by people whose remaining four senses must compensate for the loss of one. He overhears someone eavesdropping at the door - a heavy breather.

The Title: The house with such a pretentious title provides the element of mystery because an interested party makes the curious offer of buying the house replete with furnishings, down to personal items. On Holmes' advice, the bid is unacceptable.

Once he learns the reason behind the offer, he handles it to the satisfaction of all involved.

By now Doyle's affinity for numbers in his titles is obvious, and his preference for three, evident. The numbers are arbitrary. "The Five Pips" could have been three or six; "The Six Napoleons" might have been five; "The Three Students" two or four; "The Three Gables" anything but seven; "The Three Garridebs" four. Perhaps only in "The Second Stain" does it make a difference.

Holmes: The story gains most of its interest from the character of Holmes. His treatment of the black Steve Dixie may not be to his credit, but it hardly argues prejudice. Once again Holmes commutes (or more properly, commits misprision of) a felony in his dealings with the ruthless Isadora Klein with less cause than in previous cases. It does resemble blackmail on his part, but the money enables his client to travel around the world, while persecution of Miss Klein would not have accomplished this.

Vocabulary: bruiser - a professional boxer. Informal: a bully. (Holmes used the term in both senses.)

"belle dame sans merci" - a beautiful ruthless woman (French).

"THE SUSSEX VAMPIRE"

This is one of the best of the *Casebook* stories, many of which are rejected by Sherlockians as being "uncanonical" (i.e., not written by Watson). The pace is swift and the suspense heightened by the bizarre nature of the case and by Ferguson's dilemma in being torn between his love for his son and that for his wife.

Laughter: The story opens with Holmes chuckling. In spite of what Watson says of Holmes in HOUN, Holmes was far from humorless. Dr. Jay Finley Christ has noted fifty-one times when Holmes is specifically stated to have laughed in the Canon, and there are many instances of Holmes' dry and often mischievous sense of humor manifesting itself in encounters with pompous clients (MAZA, SILV, etc.).

Holmes: Typified here is Holmes' level-headed philosophy and his tact (in handling the delicate revelation of the painful truth).

Unchronicled Cases: Watson indulges in one of his favorite literary games by having Holmes mention several unchronicled cases to tantalize the reader. The best example of this trick is found in the opening of THOR.

Sensationalism: In the writing of this story, as in several of the later tales, Doyle was obviously influenced by the public taste for the sensational. It may owe its origin to Bram Stoker's *Dracula* as CREE may have been inspired by Robert Louis Stevenson's *The Strange Case of Dr. Jekyll and Mr. Hyde*.

Borrowed Devices: Doyle often borrows character types and plot tricks from other tales. The wounded dog (second "Carlo") may be compared to the sheep in SILV. Ferguson, the powerful man physically ruined by misfortune, is reminiscent of Gilchrist and Staunton in 3STU and MISS respectively; and Ferguson's fiery South American wife reminds the reader of Mrs. Gibson in THOR. The character of Jacky, however, is unique; his misguided love combined with his genius and youth make him a fascinating psychological study. Ferguson also emerges vividly, exasperated in his desperation by Holmes' reticence and deliberateness.

"THE THREE GARRIDEBS"

Crime-wise, this case is a companion piece to ENGI because it deals with counterfeiting. Its whimsical tone places it alongside BLUE, and the weird pretext used to get someone off the premises ranks it with REDH and STOC. In its classic display of Holmes' concern for Watson, it is unique.

Curiosity: Watson gains his desired effect of curiosity in the opening paragraph where he debates whether the story qualifies as a tragedy or a comedy. He tips the scales in favor of the former by listing the dire consequences that resulted, but he raises the question of a comical note.

Revelation: Holmes, the human lie-detector, quickly sizes up an American crook and, with Watson, waits for "Killer Evans" to make his move. The gangster almost lives up to his reputation, so moving as to give Holmes a terrific scare and Watson a surface wound in the thigh. Holmes was beside himself with concern for Watson, and Watson is outside of himself with ecstasy on catching "a glimpse of a great heart as well as of a great brain." What has been implicit through their years of companionship and expressed briefly in Devi, is at last made explicit.

"Killer Evans": Doyle's American gangsters are straight out of the pages of Bret Harte, so the reader is not surprised to hear Evans regret being "too soft hearted" to kill Nathan Garribed.

Knighthood: An autobiographical note in reverse creeps in when mention is made of the fact that Holmes declined the honor of knighthood in the very year that Doyle himself accepted it. The author toyed with the idea of refusing it but acquiesced to the wishes of his family, especially his mother who thought it might be considered an insult to the new king, Edward VII.

Other similarities between author and creature include their disdain for suffragettes (HISL), habit of lounging in a dressing gown, practice of keeping a revolver in their desk drawer, use of the same bank, fondness for pipes, and desire to see justice accomplished.

Vocabulary: buckboard - a light, four-wheeled, open carriage, having a long, flexible board in place of body and springs.

"THE PROBLEM OF THOR BRIDGE"

The opening of this tale contains one of the most tantalizing references to unchronicled cases in the Canon. Watson mentions several cases that are deposited in his dispatch box and the bank of Cox and Company in Charing Cross. (This bank was supposedly destroyed in WWII bombings and the fate of those manuscripts must remain forever unknown.) The cases include the disappearance of James Phillmore who, "stepping back into his own house to get his umbrella, was never more seen in this world"; the disappearance of the cutter Alicia; and the remarkable worm which drove Isadora Persano insane.

Client: Holmes has not had such an entertaining or successful encounter with a self-impressed client since the first story SCAN. Here Holmes shows himself equally skillful in putting conceited clients in their place with a few well-chosen words and a rare bluff.

Fees: Holmes seems a trifle sanctimonious when he informs Gibson that his "charges are on a fixed scale," something which is not evident in the Canon. There are cases in which the work is its own reward; and conversely, there are cases such as PRIO and 3GAB, in which Holmes accepted suspiciously large rewards (in return for silence as to certain crimes) from the Duke of Holdernesse and Isadora Klein. In view of these acceptances Holmes' comment to Gibson (that rich men have to be taught that the world cannot be bribed) sounds exaggeratedly righteous.

Suspense: Doyle utilizes his best writing skills and favorite tricks to create suspense in this tale, perhaps the best in the Casebook. Through Watson, Doyle hints at the vital clues, but has Holmes remain uncommunicative about their significance. Doyle also has the clues point a little too obviously to the wrong person - so obviously in fact that Holmes almost admits defeat in their face. Suspense builds until the last moment when Holmes realizes that he has been "sluggish in mind" and realizes the truth.

Characterization: The detailed character descriptions range from the magnificent one of the major character Gibson (whose physical appearance reflects his inner rapacity and coldness) to a very detailed and effective description of a minor character, Sergeant Coventry. Through Watson's description of the lovely Grace Dunbar, Doyle also gives us a glimpse of Watson's character, which tends to be excessively impressed by female clients and sees Miss Dunbar through the clouded eyes of a romantic.

"THE CREEPING MAN"

This maverick tale opens with a classic telegram from Holmes to Watson: "Come at once if convenient - if inconvenient come all the same." The telegram is The Holmes medium par excellence because of his concise wording, a knack that would prove as economical as it was literary.

Self-Evaluation: Watson, the understanding and patient standby of Holmes, analyzes their relationship. He classifies himself as a "habit," an "institution" like Holmes' pipe, slippers, or violin. Watson's dry sense of humor and gift for understatement make him think that many of the Master's remarks could just as appropriately have been addressed to the bedstead. The doctor, friend, partner, chronicler did recognize Holmes' need for a whetstone, someone to stimulate the Master Mind. Watson considered himself fortunate to have been destined to serve this purpose.

Dogs: In this story, Holmes' observations on the nature of dogs prove interesting in the light of his experience. They function well in his assembling of clues. In SILV, the unbarking dog indicated that the intruder was a well-known figure; in SUSS, Carlo, the limping dog, tipped Holmes off that it had been used as a guinea pig; in COPP and SHOS, the dogs turned on their masters as in this story; in CHAR, Holmes saw to it that his "fiancé" Agatha had the dog tied up; in MISS he had to use his stick against the doctor's dog but he used a dog, Pompey, to follow the scent of anisine oil which he had sprinkled on the wheel of a carriage. In LION, the fidelity of the canine creature is well proven.

Wisdom: In this Dr. Jekyll-Mr. Hyde story, Holmes has occasion to philosophize about human frailty in the memorable passage in which he comments on the possibility of a youth elixir.

Theme: Doyle provided a profound theme, expressed in Holmes' philosophy, which he illustrated poorly in this heavily Gothic tale. He selected an interesting character in Professor Presbury whose whirlwind courtship of a much younger woman creates curiosity and suspense. The sensational and macabre effects of the defective drugs subtract from the overall effect. Nathaniel Hawthorne was more successful in showing in "Dr. Heidegger's Experiment" what Holmes surmised here.

"THE LION'S MANE"

This picture of Holmes in retirement is greatly at odds with the younger Holmes complaining, "my mind rebels at stagnation." Yet four years before LION, in GREE, Holmes expressed a desire for a quiet countrified retirement.

Motivation: What brought about his change of heart and led to his early retirement from work he so loved? Did he feel that the death of Moriarty climaxed his career and that the average criminal posed no challenge? His boredom with mediocre criminality was evident from the outset. In retrospect, one can glimpse manifestations of his contemplative nature. His love of Nature (NAVA), his quiet personal study, his appreciation of the arts were noticeable even in the most pressing cases. Perhaps Holmes' travels in Tibet during the Hiatus (the period between the Reichenbach Falls incident and his return) and his contact with the Head Llama [sic] were influential in changing his hierarchy of values. Once he altered his priorities, he abandoned his rushed and harried life.

Holmes' Records: This is the second time that Holmes took pen in hand to relate a story (the other is BLAN). Instead of a cold scientific lecture (which might have been expected since he reprimanded Watson for degrading what should have been discourses into tales, in COPP), Holmes shows in writing this story a decided romantic streak second only to Watson's. What could be more romantic than Holmes' lavish praise of Maudie Bellamy, or his dramatic opening paragraph? He admits in his earlier attempt at self-chronicling that he slowly came to realize the importance of capturing the reader's attention. To achieve this end, however, he overdoes it and produces purple patches.

Dogs: Despite Holmes' fondness for dogs, they do not receive kind treatment in the Canon. The hound of the Baskervilles and Carlo (COPP) were shot; Lady Brackenstall's dog was set afire (ABBE); Ferguson's dog and the ailing pup of Mrs. Hudson were poisoned (SUSS, STUD); Watson's bull-pup met an unknown end (STUD); and here McPherson's dog is brutally thrown through a window.

Doyle: In a *Strand* article, Doyle admitted that having Holmes tell the story himself tended to cramp the narrative. What suffers is the ease that normally characterizes the concealment of truth until the final dramatic disclosure. Ordinarily, Holmes kept his own personal theories from Watson; here, he deliberately withholds them from the reader, which is less forgivable. While Doyle held a high opinion of the plot, readers tend to be more impressed with the fascinating glimpse of Holmes in retirement. The surprise at the end is satisfactorily bizarre but fails to provide adequate satisfaction on second reading. Holmes is admittedly slow in making deduction, and discovers the true answer only through a stroke of luck.

Weapon: Doyle might have made a better choice of a murder weapon had he used the "Cyanea Arctica" rather than its cousin, the "Cyanea Capillita"; the latter could hardly inflict such dreadful injuries as befell McPherson and Murdoch.

"THE VEILED LODGER"

This tale gives Holmes no chance to display his talents as detective, but it reveals him as a philosopher and man.

Holmes: Holmes here is more than a thinking machine - he is a philosopher and humanist. His sympathetic nature and firm convictions are clearly revealed in the last scene in which he convinces Mrs. Ronder not to commit suicide. His philosophies on the afterlife in this story are like his musings in BOSC and CARD. Occasionally, the cruelty of Fate depresses Holmes to an abnormal point (often forcing him to seek solace in drugs); see BOSC and RETI. Yet his sympathetic character makes him aware of life's importance and he convinces Mrs. Ronder that her life is not her own. This is Holmes, the man, at his best.

"Filthy Habit": When Holmes refers to Watson's smoking as a "filthy habit" it is surely with tongue-in-cheek. Watson was usually reprimanding Holmes on his addiction to the "weed" in various forms.

Unchronicled: The mention of "the story concerning the politician, the lighthouse and the trained cormorant" is one of the most tantalizing references in the Canon. **Realism** is added to the story by Watson's threat to make the story known if further attempts to destroy his manuscripts are made. Could that "one reader" have been successful in destroying the manuscripts so that none of the unchronicled cases mentioned in the published cases were ever published? Or did these attempts at vandalism force Watson to transfer his papers to the vault at the Cox and Company Bank (THOR)?

Sensationalism: The story continues in the "sensational" vein in which many of the later stories were written. In the *Casebook* tales, Holmes often ceases to be the focal point, and some sensational or grotesque plot device becomes central (the mutilation of Mrs. Ronder in this case; leprosy in BLAN; a deranged child in SUSS; a Jekyll-Hyde transformation in CREE, etc.). There seems little need for Holmes' presence in this tale, despite the vivid characterization of him as philosopher. Apparently, Doyle's well of creativity was running dry with regard to Holmes, and he allowed the public demand for the bizarre to influence him in later tales.

"SHOSCOMBE OLD PLACE"

One of the better *Casebook* tales, this story succeeds in portraying Holmes as the scientific detective, bent over the microscope as the story opens. (One of his many successors will be Dr. Thorndyke, created by R. Austin Freeman, whose Red Thumb-Mark shows an indebtedness to NORW with its forged fingerprint.)

Watson: Holmes cuts an imposing figure at the end as he masterfully controls and reprimands Sir Robert. Watson, on the other hand, makes a poor showing when he displays ignorance of the anatomical niceties by identifying a piece of bone as "the upper condoyle of a human femur," which does not even exist; when he admits being a victim of gambling fever and losing a good deal of money to the racetracks (he has come a long way from his ignorance of racing in Silv); and when he appears to be socially prejudiced by expressing doubt that a man of Sir Robert's station could be a criminal (despite his experience with Sir George Burnwell [BERY] and Count Sylvius [MAZA], among others).

Plot: Doyle gives the reader a swift-moving mystery with a unique plot composed of several puzzling elements, all of which tie in neatly at the end. Characterization and description are minimal, but the story avoids the encumbrance which might have resulted from so much detail in two ways: First, sparkling dialogue conveys the information vital to the plot. Second, suspense is kindled and rekindled by the way Doyle alternates scenes of suspense. Holmes' mysterious experiment with the black spaniel and the final nocturnal visit to the crypt produce atmospheric pressure that leads up to a climactic confrontation between Holmes and Sir Robert with the revelation of the corpse. The fact that this tale centers around gambling also heightens the suspense. Note Holmes' many references to gambling, especially card metaphors.

"THE RETIRED COLOURMAN"

This is one of those cases that build to interesting heights from unlikely beginnings. Usually, though, when Inspector Hopkins sends a case Holmes' way, there is something to it and this is no exception.

Foreshadowing: Watson qualifies as the founder of the "had I but known" school when he anticipates the eventual outcome: "The case will be the eager debate of all England." In DANC, he writes: "Would that I had some brighter ending" to "the chain of events which for some days made the Ridling Thorpe Manor a household word." (Mary Roberts Rinehart made this one of the features of her detective novels.)

Watson: As in HOUN and DISA, Watson does some reconnoitering for Holmes but returns with isolated facts that necessitate Holmes' visiting the scene to supply missing links. Listening to Watson, Holmes shows impatience at his poetic embellishments. When Watson remarks that he never noticed Amberley's artificial limb, the tone of Holmes' answer can only be inferred.

Credit: Although put out with Watson's shortcomings, Holmes lavishes praise on him whenever it is deserved. He informs Inspector MacKinnon that his "astute friend" noticed a number that was an important clue.

Trickery: Holmes had wide experience with maneuvers to keep people off certain premises by having them perform ridiculous tasks elsewhere (remember REDH and STOC) and he makes use of Watson to keep Amberley entertained. Although this seems to be taking advantage of Watson, he is game. The client foolishly underestimated the ability of Holmes who was quick to smell a rat even though fresh paint had been applied.

Dying Words: It is proverbial that a man's dying words are important. In the possibility of murder, this is doubly true. In Doyle's stories, those last words are usually suspense-getters, rarely understood until the great Mind interprets them in their proper context. In BOSC, "rat" on the lips of Charles McCarthy was little or no help until Holmes recognized it as one syllable of a place in Australia. In SPEC, the words "speckled band" misled Holmes until the end. In GOLD, the words "it was she" made a little more sense. In this story, "We we..." is puzzling. Why would a dying man attempt a complete sentence when the single word, "murdered" would have done? Apparently, he was attempting, "We were murdered."

Holmes' Reference Books: Holmes consults his Crockford's Clerical Directory for the name of J. C. Elman. Also on his shelf were the *American Encyclopedia* (FIVE) which scholars claim must have been *The International Cyclopedia*; *The Gazetteer of the World* (SCAN); the London Telephone Directory (3GAR); a journal of his cuttings (ENGI); and a "red-covered volume" for genealogical information which must have been a Debrett (NOBL). His library must have included the Bible, Shakespeare, Horace, Petrarch, and Meredith.

Finale: While this tale is not bad, one cannot help but wish for a more suitable finale to Holmes' published career. If it would not deprive readers of a few gems like SUSS and THOR, one almost wishes that Doyle had quit with the superbly dramatic and appropriate HISL. Perhaps like Stevenson and other authors, he could have requested that this particular story always be printed at the end of his works.

Vocabulary: colorman - a dealer in paints or dyes.

CHARACTER ANALYSES

SHERLOCK HOLMES

Sherlock Holmes has often been listed among the most famous literary characters ever created; the word "sherlock" has become a synonym for detective; and surely, the image of the tall, spare, hook-nosed figure with Inverness cape, magnifying glass, deerstalker cap, and pipe (an image fostered more by the movie industry than by Doyle's writings) is familiar to people everywhere. Just what are the characteristics which make Holmes so popular?

INTELLECTUAL QUALITIES

Holmes said of himself in MAZA: "I am a brain; the rest of me is a mere appendix." He is, first and foremost, the rational animal, the problem-solver. Through careful training and self-discipline he has taught himself the delicate art of observation; he notes the smallest details and deduces so much from them that he elevates deductive reasoning to an art. He is an expert scientist in fields which aid him in criminal investigation; and he is equally expert in specialized areas which are important only in his profession (e.g., distinguishing tobacco ash or recognizing various types of ears, both subjects of Holmes monographs).

The basis of his theory, which was based upon the observance of trifles and the inference of what lay beyond them, was outlined by Holmes himself in his article "The Book of Life" in STUD.

EMOTIONAL QUALITIES

Early in their partnership, Watson says of Holmes that all emotions were abhorrent to him. Yet here Watson underrated Holmes; Holmes was not without emotions, only in control of them. Although it was plain from the outset (SCAN) that there was no room for a love affair, Holmes was no misogynist and did not dislike women as Watson asserted. Witness Holmes' regard for Irene Adler (SCAN), Mrs. Ronder (VEIL), Violet Hunter (COPP), etc., and his chivalrous treatment of women. It is perhaps true that he distrusted women; but after encounters with persons such as Irene Adler, Isadora Klein (3GAB) and the woman who poisoned her children (SIGN), who can blame him? He was not trusting of men, either; Holmes had few if any friends (other than Watson), feeling that love or friendship would bias his judgment. His aloofness was a deliberate facade and the result of self-training; but that emotions did stir within him is evident on occasions when he shows concern for Watson (most notably 3GAR) and for clients (Openshaw and Cubitt) whose deaths he could not prevent.

Aesthetic Aspects: Holmes was a sensitive person who appreciated "finer things." He enjoyed good music and was himself no mean violinist. Although he often fasted to save time and sharpen his mental faculties while on a case, he relished a gourmet meal. His library was extensive. It seems probable that rare book collecting was among his outside interests, and he read on topics ranging from sensational crime to philosophy.

Philosophy: Holmes' evolution as a philosopher throughout the Canon is interesting; while Watson originally says that he had no interest in nature (STUD), it gradually became apparent that the Sussex downs had become more acceptable to Holmes' taste than the London streets. By FINA his leaning towards nature was quite pronounced. Eventually, he retired to a life of nature and bee-keeping in Sussex.

Holmes was fascinated by mankind in general and especially the interrelation of man with nature and Fate. He is acutely aware of how small a twist of Fate is necessary to alter an entire life. In STUD Holmes wrote an article stating his belief that everything in the world is interrelated and that a true logician could "infer the possibility of an Atlantic" from a drop of water. As Holmes says in NAVA, deduction is especially necessary in religion; in the same story he deduces the existence of God from a rose.

Need For Stimulation: Holmes' philosophizing on the state of the world often drove him into the deepest depression from which he could only be aroused by mental diversion and stimulation. Beside his desire to help his fellow man, his need for stimulation drove him, producing the fierce energy that he employs in detective work. When criminals are unoriginal and dull and no mental stimulant is forthcoming, he turns to artificial ones - cocaine or morphine. He says in REDH that his life is a sustained effort to escape the commonplace. Perhaps this is the key to his personality.

Drama: If as Walpole said, "The world is a comedy to those who think, a tragedy to those who feel," then Holmes' witty cynicism, fondness for drama, and enjoyment of practical jokes seem characteristic (although at times he felt the tragedy of the world keenly). His quest for justice, not only the justice of

English law, but of a "higher court," was his attempt to alleviate some of the wrongs of the world. He is a fine actor and expert at disguise; while these are very helpful to him in his work, they are also another attempt to escape the common place.

Detachment: The supreme manifestation of Holmes' omnipotent logic is his almost oriental power of detachment. When he can do no more for a time in an investigation, he does not worry about it but allows his mind to relax and dwell on other subjects. In London, it is violin concerts; in Cornwall or the Baskerville moors, ancient rock-dwellings.

Eccentricities: His very eccentricities fill out his image. A typical Victorian bachelor, he indulges freely in his eccentric pleasures which include indoor target-practice, smoking large amounts of shag (kept in a Persian slipper), fixing his unanswered mail with a jackknife to the mantel, and littering his rooms with papers in a fashion uncharacteristic of his organized mind (which apparently is taken up with more important matters). Social functions and manners bore him; yet he can be charming when it suits his purpose. His Bohemian nature is representative of the Bohemian richness of the Victorian life-tapestry. His peculiarities are outlets for his precise mind; and those which may be labeled "weaknesses" serve another practical purpose by showing that he is not infallible. This makes him more credible and likable to the reader. He made mistakes (FIVE), was temporarily tricked by red herrings (SPEC), and often felt that he had done more harm in capturing criminals than they had done by their crimes (BLUE). Egocentric as he often appears, Holmes is in reality humble, for humility is truth; and he was not blind to his merits or his defects. He did not rank modesty among the virtues (GREE).

Appeal: It is probably his superhuman mental capacity, couched as it is in human weakness and eccentricities, that makes him such a popular character. Also engaging is the nostalgic way in which Doyle depicts the age. Rex Stout called Holmes "human aspiration...what our ancestors had in mind when in wistful braggadocio they tacked the sapiens onto the homo... He is human as a man but not as a detective." William Bolitho called him "the spirit of a town and a time." Doyle's brother-in-law, E. W. Hornung, punned, "Though he might be more humble, there's no police like Holmes." But Edgar Smith, the great Sherlockian, summed it up best when he said that Holmes was "...a symbol of all that we are not, but ever would be...bringing high adventure to our dull existence and calm judicial logic to our biased mind. He is the success of all our failures; the bold escape from our imprisonment..." He is Sherlock Holmes!

Watson: For all of his constant and invaluable importance in the Canon, Watson remains one of its most unappreciated characters. While "Sherlock Holmes" is used as a synonym for a clever reasoner, rarely is "John Watson" used to mean the most loyal of friends, most understanding of doctors, most dedicated of chroniclers, and most patient of men.

Biography: As with Holmes, little is known about Watson's life but much is discerned about his character. It is generally (but by no means unanimously) agreed that he was born in South England in 1852, attended one of the better English public schools, and spent some time in Australia before taking his Doctor of Medicine degree at the University of London in 1878. The tale of his service as Army Surgeon and subsequent wounding at Maiwand and return to England are related in STUD.

Marriages: One of the most puzzling questions about Watson, is how many times was he married? In SIGN, Watson, with a modesty and naivete bespeaking a first deep romantic interest, wooed and won Mary Morstan. In EMPT, Holmes speaks of Watson's bereavement, apparently Mary's death. In BLAN (1903) Holmes comments that "the good Watson had at that time deserted me for a wife, the only selfish action which I can recall in our association." After a long retirement from private practice during which he returned to Baker Street, Watson again bought a practice, this time on Queen Anne Street and again settled down with a wife. So much is fairly straightforward, but the Canon is full of chronological references to Watson's marriages which are so contradictory in nature that they seem to indicate that Watson was married more than twice. Perhaps Watson's later wife (or wives) did not take as kindly as Mary to those summonses of Holmes which often called Watson from his practice and home at an earlier period. Watson was notoriously inaccurate in terms of dating anyway, and it may be best to leave well enough alone, grant him two wives, and not join what Dorothy Sayers called "the conspiracy to provide Watson with as many wives as Henry VIII."

Romantic: Watson was by nature a romantic; Holmes often accused him of embellishing the cold facts of deduction into fanciful tales and Watson is often guilty of purple prose (especially when describing Holmes' female clients). In one of the few immodest statements Watson makes, he admits that he has had worldwide experience with women (SIGN). Watson is also fond of romantic adventure in another sense of the word; his willingness to join Holmes in any adventure, no matter how dangerous, indicates not only loyalty to Holmes but a love of adventure for adventure's sake. Holmes says that Watson shares his "love of all that is bizarre."

Loyalty: Despite constant barbs, sarcasm, and criticism which would have made a lesser man flinch, Watson remains forever loyal to Holmes throughout the Canon. He endured the most heinous of deceptions on Holmes' part (EMPT and DYIN) good-naturedly. He nursed Holmes through the throes of drug addiction and eventually broke him of the habit. He was ready to join Holmes in any danger, unwilling to leave Holmes alone when in danger, ready even to accompany Holmes on a life-and-death flight to the Continent at a moment's notice (FINA).

Doctor And Chronicler: Watson had a natural sympathy and interest in his fellow man which made him a thoughtful doctor with, no doubt, an excellent bedside manner. He was too much of a romantic, however, to find his practice absorbing when there was a chance of adventure with Holmes; neither must he have found medical journals very absorbing, for in several cases he makes a glaringly obvious medical faux pas. However, a doctor is certainly a valuable companion for a detective! As chronicler, Holmes accuses him of romanticizing and yet admits "I am lost without my Boswell." (The comparison to Boswell is appropriate, for like Boswell, Watson carefully chronicles every gem of wisdom that falls from the Master's lips, at the same time offering interesting insights into himself through his writing.)

Average? Surely Watson is the epitome of average English manhood. His loyalty and romantic sense of honor may be far above average, but still Watson is the Victorian common man, someone with whom every reader can identify. In the face of Sherlock's superhuman logic, a reader needs another character with whom he can share his bafflement and exasperation. Holmes alone would be intolerable.

Friend: It is his characteristic modesty, willingness to help, and loyalty which make Watson what he is above all: the archetypal friend. Good old Watson!

PROFESSOR MORIARTY

Called by many critics the "greatest villain in literature," Professor Moriarty is certainly the only villain to approach being Holmes' intellectual equal. Doyle created Moriarty as an assassin for Holmes when he planned FINA to be the last Holmes story. As such, Moriarty must be Holmes' equal, in every respect, but not his superior, for this would be an admission that evil can ultimately triumph over good.

Moriarty is Holmes' antithesis, his alter-ego, his Mr. Hyde. They are physically similar: tall, thin, ascetic-looking, to emphasize their intellectual equality. Their conversation in FINA is a masterpiece of give-and-take, with each preserving his well-deserved reputation with neither quite attaining the upper hand. When they supposedly went over that cliff into Reichenbach Falls, it was together - with neither Good nor Evil triumphing and both retaining a perfect balance to the last, an idea which would certainly have appealed to Doyle's spiritualist mind.

Like Holmes, Moriarty is a genius, a philosopher, and an abstract thinker. Moriarty won a prominent position in the academic world through several writings which were the product of his amazing mathematical faculty; he used his prominence and facade of respectability as a front for his underworld operations. Holmes' comparison of Moriarty to a gigantic spider with threads extending throughout the criminal world of London is apt; and his description and brief biography of Moriarty in FINA is far more detailed than any which can be given here.

Three facts about Moriarty raise him above the normal criminal level to the position of "Napoleon of Crime." First, his mental equality with Holmes makes him as much a symbol of Evil as Holmes is of Good. It is from Moriarty that Holmes receives his greatest challenge and stimulation (in FINA and VALL); after FINA Holmes will often complain of the lack of originality and challenge in the criminal world since the death of Professor Moriarty. Secondly, his quiet self-assurance makes him the epitome of Doyle's favorite type of villain, the "quiet" villain - one whose bite is so deadly that his bark need not be loud. Finally, Moriarty is frightening because of the careful way in which he has protected himself. He only plans, committing no actual crime himself; should the real criminal be caught, his actions will never be traced to Moriarty. This makes Moriarty unreachable, unconquerable to all but Holmes, and it is at the Master's hands that this Napoleon meets his Waterloo.

THE INSPECTORS

In the short stories appear eight Scotland Yard Inspectors (Baynes, Bradstreet, Forrester, Gregory, Gregson, Hopkins, Lanner, and Lestrade); Barker, a private investigator; Leverton of the Pinkerton Agency; and the "other detective." Of these, only three warrant characterization: Gregson, Hopkins, and Lestrade.

TOBIAS GREGSON

Holmes thought highly of this tall, white-faced, flaxen-haired inspector. More characterization is given of him in the novels than in the three short stories, GREE, REDC, and WIST. Watson refers to him as robust and official-looking. There is proof of his courage in REDC where he insists quietly on being the first inspector to apprehend a dangerous criminal, calmly at that. Whenever he imagines that he has beaten Holmes to a clue or conclusion, he is genuinely proud. He is represented as an energetic, gallant, and capable officer. He appreciates Holmes' help and cooperates fully.

STANLEY HOPKINS

Although Holmes mentions seven cases sent him by Hopkins, only four are on record; BLAC, GOLD, MISS, and ABBE. In BLAC, Watson places the young inspector in his early thirties. Obviously, he was enterprising and strove to imitate Holmes in his modus operandi. Even though instructed by the Master, Hopkins lacked the intuitive ability that might have saved his painstaking methods from futility. He fails to observe the Master's injunction to consider every possible alternative. Unable to imagine alternatives, he accepts the obvious as conclusive. He is humble and takes with good grace the sarcasm leveled at him by his instructor.

G. LESTRADE

Of all the inspectors, Lestrade is the best known and most likable, appearing in eleven short stories and two novels. Watson almost over-emphasizes his small stature. His attitude toward Holmes approaches scorn in BOSC when he calls Holmes to task for raising the hopes of a young woman in such a hopeless case. The Master scolds Lestrade vitriolically in the same case.

Like Gregson, Lestrade is jubilant when he thinks he has found something overlooked by the Expert. While there is an interesting bit of professional rivalry between the two inspectors, neither resents Holmes. Lestrade is practical, down-to-earth, and occasionally impatient with the inscrutable Holmes. He adds a vein of humor when he gestures to Watson that Holmes is touched in the head. Energetic, excitable, and unimaginative, he is the no-nonsense official. He pays Holmes one of the finest compliments in the Canon (NORW), assuring him that every man at Scotland Yard would feel proud to shake his hand. According to Holmes, Gregson and Lestrade are the "best pick of a bad lot." They serve as foils and rivals for Holmes to add an extra touch of humor and suspense.

MYCROFT HOLMES

Watson cannot resist lengthy descriptions of the man's enormity: his "portly form," "unwieldy frame," "gross body"; but first impressions are not lasting once the man's dominant mind becomes evident. His masterful brow, deep-set, steel-grey eyes and firm lips testify to mental ability and will power that are in direct contrast to the "suggestion of uncouth physical inertia in the figure." His size and deliberate speech might remind one of Sidney Greenstreet.

Sherlock seems pleased to be able to show his brother off to Watson, engaging him in a verbal contest of an observational and deductive nature to Mycroft's advantage. Sherlock explains that his older brother lacks the physical energy to test his convictions or follow up on them. The least effort would prove too taxing for such a phlegmatic man.

Mycroft is a creature of habit, sedentary at that. His appearance at 221B Baker Street makes Sherlock compare it to a planet leaving its orbit. Nevertheless, Mycroft has become a founder-member of an anti-clubbing club for those who desire peace and quiet. His steady, dependable nature makes him a valuable asset in his government position. Sherlock admits that Mycroft has no ambition, but he cannot deny that sometimes his brother Is the British government.

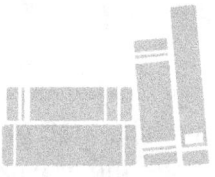

CRITICISM

ON DETECTIVE FICTION, HOLMES, AND WATSON

Detective fiction has always been a neglected stepchild of literature - neglected by critics, that is, and kept in its place by publishers. Readers, however, have always been faithful in tremendous number to their favorite sleuths from Sherlock Holmes to Nero Wolfe to Sam Spade to Lew Archer.

- Raymond A. Sokolov

...from the outset, detection has always been written for and by highbrows.

- Jacques Barzun

For me, as for many others, the reading of detective stories is an addiction like tobacco or alcohol.

- W. H. Auden

It would be foolish to deny that detection in literature submits to very rigid canons. It is an art of symmetry, it seeks the appearance of logical necessity, like classical tragedy, and like tragedy, it cherishes the unity of place.... Its successes thus partake of the tour de force.... What do we gain from the details of detection? An understanding, first, of the silent life of things, and next, of the spectacle of mind at work. This is no doubt why detective feats have been....delights of intellectuals. The emotion called forth is that of seeing order grow out of confusion.... The supreme quality in our special **genre**, is, of course, invention, which is to say, imagination.

    - Jacques Barzun

It [the detective story] is the earliest and only form of popular literature in which is expressed some sense of the poetry of modern life.

    - G. K. Chesterton

The rules of art are as much involved in this artistic form as in any other.

    - G. K. Chesterton

Future literary historians may pass somewhat lightly over the compositions of the "serious" novelists and turn their attention to the immense and varied achievement of the detective writers.

    - Somerset Maugham

Finger printing and chemical analysis have sent hundreds of our older detective stories into discard. Nothing so makes a detective story appear outmoded so much as the employment of elaborate scientific methods. Simplicity of means, valid characters, and distinguished writing are the qualities that best enable crime fiction to defy the ravages of time.

- Philip Van Doren Stern

If I were choosing the best twenty stories, at least one half dozen would be about Sherlock Holmes.

- Julian Symonds

In 1887 A Study in Scarlet was flung like a bombshell into the field of detective fiction, to be followed within a few short and brilliant years by the marvelous series of Sherlock Holmes short stories. The effect was electric. Conan Doyle took up the Poe formula and galvanized it into life and popularity.

- Dorothy Sayers

People say that Sherlock Holmes is the most widely known fictional character in all the literature of the world, and there is impressive evidence that they are right.... Sherlock Holmes is the embodiment of man's greatest pride and greatest weakness: his reason. I have heard it said by sneerers that he wasn't even human. Certainly he wasn't; but he is human aspiration. He is what our ancestors had in mind when in wistful braggadocio they tacked the sapiens onto the homo.... He is human as a man but not as a detective. He is human when he plays the violin or gets impatient with Watson, or puts his tobacco in an old Persian slipper, but not when he glances at a bit of ash and knows the name of the cigar it came from. Then he is a flaming realization of man's most ambitious dream and no character in a dream is human.

- Rex Stout

The most characteristic of Holmes' everyday phrases carry Dr. Watson's name down the corridors of fame and are today familiar to everybody, everywhere. Who has not heard, "Elementary, my dear Watson"? Who has not thrilled to the immortal call to mystery and adventure, "Come, Watson, come! The game is afoot"?

- C. Blegan and W. N. McDiarmid

Sherlock Holmes is as fully a character as Mr. Pickwick. And by virtue of Doyle's almost unique success in giving a soul to the detective's partner - the common man - we have in the two a companion pair to Don Quixote and Sancho Panza, a contrast and concert capable of occupying our imagination apart from the tales in which the two figure.

- Jacques Barzun

Every detective story writer makes mistakes, of course, and none will ever know so much as he should. Conan Doyle made mistakes which completely invalidated some of his stories, but he was a pioneer and Sherlock Holmes after all is mostly an attitude, and a few dozen lines of unforgettable dialogue.

- Raymond Chandler

What one loves in Holmes, in truth, is not his logic but his habits and his colleague.

- E. M. Wrong

And we can all be thankful that Dr. Watson wrote as he did: half the fun in reading and re-reading the Saga is that of catching him out - as generations of his admirers have been discovering for more than three quarters of a century now.

- William S. Baring-Gould

There is no Sherlockian worth his salt who has not, at least once in his life, taken Dr. Watson's pen in hand and given himself to the production of a veritable adventure.... The writing of a pastiche is compulsive and inevitable; it is, the psychologists say, a wholesome manifestation of the urge that is in us all to return to the times and places we have loved and lost....

- Edgar W. Smith

What is it that we love in Sherlock Holmes? We love the times in which he lived, of course, the half-remembered, half-forgotten times of snug Victorian illusion, of gaslit comfort and contentment, of perfect dignity and grace. The world was poised precariously in balance.... But there is more than the time and space and the yearning for things gone by to account for what we feel toward Sherlock Holmes. Not only there and then, but here and now, he stands before us as a symbol - a symbol of all that we are not, but ever would be.... He is Galahad and Socrates, bringing high adventure to our dull existence and calm, judicial logic to our biased mind. He is the success of all our failures; the bold escape from our imprisonment.

- Edgar W. Smith

Let no man write his **epitaph**. He is not dead.

- John Dickson Carr

...they still live for all that love them well: in a romantic chamber of the heart: in a nostalgic country of the mind, where it is always 1895.

- Vincent Starrett

ESSAY QUESTIONS AND ANSWERS

Question: How Was Doyle Influenced By Edgar Allan Poe?

Answer: Doyle was much indebted to Poe, the "Father of the Detective Story." Poe was the first to produce the brilliant, eccentric amateur detective whose admiring friend recorded their adventures. C. Auguste Dupin and his English counterpart preferred to work in the dark by candlelight even during the day. Both men used and demonstrated the deductive method of reasoning. Both had the habit of surprising their friend by "reading his mind" and then explaining how the conclusion was reached through a series of associations. Both sleuths made it their practice to estimate the caliber of their opponent's intellect in order to put themselves in that person's place and predict the next move. Attention has been called to the similarity of the meeting between the famous literary pairs: detective and companion.

Both chroniclers frequently employ a clever or appropriate epigram at an important part of the story or to summarize the case at the end. Such proverbs are usually in French or Latin, but Holmes translates them into English, occasionally.

Although Holmes indicates disdain for Dupin by calling him an "inferior fellow" although a "close reasoner," Doyle showed his esteem for Poe by imitating and improving upon certain features of the tale. Doyle does not get involved in lengthy philosophical asides that slow the narrative and tend to bore the reader.

The Paris Police and the Inspectors of Scotland Yard serve as foils for the sleuths and profit in the end by having the criminals identified and/or delivered into their hands.

Question: Describe The Role Of Watson

Answer: John H. Watson, M.D., functions effectively in several roles: (1) chronicler; (2) foil; (3) best friend and confidant; and (4) doctor.

By telling the story in the first person, the narrator gains immediacy and credibility. Holmes refers to Watson as his "Boswell" and sometimes chides him for embellishing the tales. By referring to previous cases (some real, some imaginary), the narrator can arouse the reader's curiosity, spark interest, and give the air of selectivity when he claims that he records only the unusual cases. Each case then promises to be unique in some respect.

Secondly, Watson serves as a foil for the supersleuth. He is average, prudent, quiet. He is the common man, the reader, who receives the clues along with the detective. Holmes often comments, "Watson, you know my method." Yes, Watson, and the reader as well, know the deductive method of reaching a conclusion, but he cannot apply the method to the case in hand. Watson, and often the reader, must have the individual facts connected and the conclusion explained. Where the reader is a few steps ahead of Watson, he is close on the heels of Holmes.

Third, Watson works as a humanizing agent for the eccentric intellectual. Holmes appreciates Watson's company, invites him to stay and listen to the client's story. He airs his views and solicits Watson's. Confiding in his friend, Holmes lays the clues before the reader and then explains their implications for his friend's benefit.

Rarely does Dr. Watson have occasion to utilize his medical knowledge, but on occasion he gives Dr. Doyle an opportunity to show his medical background. In several cases, a patient seeking Watson also needed Holmes (MANW, ENGI).

Question: Trace The Evolution Of The Holmes Image In The Media

Answer: Doyle drew the broad outline of Sherlock Holmes in the first work in which he appeared, *A Study in Scarlet*. Watson describes him:

> **In height he was rather over six feet, and so excessively thin that he seemed to be considerably taller. His eyes were sharp and piercing...and his thin hawk-like nose gave his whole expression an air of alertness and decision. His chin, too, had the prominence and squareness which mark the man of determination.**

Although D. H. Friston was the first to illustrate Holmes when he did the Study, it was Sidney Paget who imprinted the indelible image on the English mind. By mistake, the editors of the *Strand Magazine* commissioned Sidney, instead of his brother, Walter. Fortunately, Sidney used his brother for his model and had him wear the deerstalker cap and Inverness cape, which became hallmarks of the world's most famous detective. Paget illustrated the Adventures, the Memoirs, the Hound, and the Return. Doyle never intended Holmes to be as handsome as Paget made him, but he admitted that it proved an advantage because the Strand gained more female readers as a result. Paget's successors followed the tradition he had established.

On the stage, the American William Gillette played the part of the lean, sinewy figure to perfection with his quiet, histrionic method. He became for Americans the living embodiment of the fictional character.

Gillette found it difficult to enunciate with a straight pipe between his lips and substituted the foremost insignia of Holmes: the curved calabash. Booth Tarkington claimed that he would rather have seen Gillette play the part of Holmes than be a child again at Christmas.

What Sidney Paget did for the *Strand* in England, Frederick Dorr Steele accomplished for *Collier's Weekly* in America. He said, "I did not need to be told to make my Sherlock look like Gillette. The thing was inevitable. I kept him in mind and even copied or adapted parts of a few stage photographs." Vincent Starrett insisted, "No one can touch Steele in making you feel what is going on behind the door."

Holmes was the first detective to star in silent films. In 1903, Sherlock Holmes Baffled was produced, but because dialogue is so vital to the Holmes characterization, silent films did an injustice to him. More movies may have been made with Holmes than with any other detective, since many used only the character of Holmes with an original story. Seventeen versions of *The Hound of the Baskervilles* alone have been produced. The Dane, Forrest Holger-Madsen, was the first actor to play the part.

English actors who made names for themselves in the role were Ellie Norwood, Arthur Wontner, and Peter Cushing. American actors include John Barrymore, Clive Brook, and most popular of all, Basil Rathbone with Nigel Bruce co-starring as Watson.

On radio, the voices of Basil Rathbone, Sir John Gielgud, and Sir Cedric Hardwicke have enthralled listeners.

Series of Holmes' films have been featured on television, especially on the late shows and on PBS.

Question: What Are Some Of The Similarities Between Holmes And Doyle?

Answer: At one point in his life, Conan Doyle said, "If any man is Holmes, I confess it is myself." Both men had an insatiable thirst for justice, and won renown as criminologists. Doyle spent time, money, and energy working on the cases of Oscar Slater and George Edalji. Although Holmes was modeled on Dr. Joseph Bell, Bell protested that in reality, Holmes was Doyle in his reasoning powers. Certainly Doyle had to think through the solutions credited to the sleuth.

Biographically, the two men claimed descent from "country squires"; they both had French blood as well as artistic blood in their veins.

Doyle and Holmes shared an affinity for clay pipes and dressing gowns; they were in the habit of working up to fifteen hours a day on special projects. Each kept a magnifying glass atop his desk and a revolver in his desk drawer.

They shared dislikes also. Neither man cared for publicity nor irresponsible reporting in the press. Both were loath to accept titles; in 1902 knighthood was offered the two men for services rendered the government. Doyle felt obligated to accept for fear of offending the King, but Holmes declined. Both men disapproved of the suffragettes. Holmes referred to them as "window-breaking Furies" and Doyle supposedly told an American reporter that in their case, he approved of lynching. English suffragettes poured vitriol in his mailbox.

According to their friends, both men were good listeners. Both saw in nature proof of a provident Deity. Both believed in an afterlife and did not fear death.

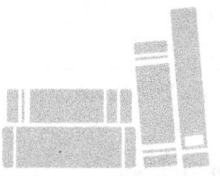

TOPICS FOR FURTHER STUDY

Holmes The Holmesian Method

Holmes' Sense of Humor

Holmes and Music

Holmes' Philosophy

Holmes' Religion

Holmes' Use of Quotations

Watson Watson's Wounds

Watson's Marriages

Watson's Dating of Cases

The Canon Blackmail in the Canon

Nemesis in the Canon

Unusual Villains in the Canon

Unusual Clients in the Canon

Scotland Yard in the Canon

Nautical Elements in the Canon

Unchronicled Cases

Doyle Influences on Doyle

Doyle and Spiritualism

Doyle's Use of Animals

Doyle's Style

Doyle and Science Fiction

Doyle's Historical Novels

Doyle's Influence on the Detective Story

BIBLIOGRAPHY

SELECTED EDITIONS OF HOLMES

Baring-Gould, William S., ed.: *The Annotated Sherlock Holmes*. New York: Clarkson N. Potter Inc., 1962. A Sherlockian's dream in two volumes, with many of the original illustrations, maps, explanations of obscure terms, and informative articles on various aspects of the Canon.

Doyle, Arthur Conan: *The Complete Sherlock Holmes*. New York: Doubleday, Doran & Co., 1930.

_____ *Sherlock Holmes: The Complete Short Stories*. and *Sherlock Holmes: The Complete Long Stories*. London: John Murray, 1929. The standard American and English editions, respectively; the Doubleday edition contains an excellent introduction by Sherlockian Christopher Morley.

SELECTED BIOGRAPHIES OF DOYLE

Carr, John Dickson: *The Life of Sir Arthur Conan Doyle*. New York: Harper & Bros., 1949. The standard biography by another famous mystery writer.

Doyle, Adrian Conan: *The True Conan Doyle*. New York: Coward-McCann, 1946. A short but more intimate view by the author's son; concentrates heavily on the Holmes stories.

Doyle, Sir Arthur Conan: *Memories and Adventures*. Boston: Little, Brown & Co., 1924. His autobiography; a classic.

Weil-Nordon, Pierre: *Sir Arthur Conan Doyle*. London: John Murray, Ltd., 1959. Offers a critical review of Doyle's work as well as interesting biographical details; especially fascinating for delving into the relationships between Holmes and his creator.

SHERLOCKIANA

Anthologies

Bell, H. W.: *Baker Street Studies*. Morristown, N.J.: The Baker Street Irregulars, Inc., 1955. Eight essays by great Sherlockians including Vincent Starrett, Dorothy Sayers, and Bell himself.

Holroyd, James Edward: *Seventeen Steps to 221B. London*: George Allen & Unwin Ltd., 1967. Seventeen essays by famous Sherlockians.

Starrett, Vincent: 221B: *Studies in Sherlock Holmes*. New York: The Macmillan Company, 1940. An anthology of essays by famous American Sherlockians including Morley, Bell, and the Holmes illustrator, Frederick Dorr Steele.

Smith, Edgar W.: *Profile by Gaslight*. New York: Simon & Schuster, 1944. A large volume of essays and verse with much material about the Baker Street Irregulars.

Single Authors

Baring-Gould, William S.: *Sherlock Holmes of Baker Street: A Life of the World's First Consulting Detective*. New York: Bramhall House, 1962. A fanciful but entertaining attempt to pad the Holmes' saga; includes a detailed chronology of cases.

Bell, H. W.: *Sherlock Holmes and Dr. Watson: The Chronology of Their Adventures.* Morristown, N.J.: The Baker Street Irregulars Inc., 1953. A first attempt to date all of Holmes' cases.

Blakeney, T. S.: *Sherlock Holmes: Fact or Fiction?* Morristown, N.J.: Baker Street Irregulars Inc., 1954. A chronology and collection of interesting essays.

Brend, Gavin: *My Dear Holmes.* London: George Allen & Unwin Ltd., 1951. A collection of essays on various Canonical characters and aspects of Holmes' life with entertaining personal touches and a chronology.

Carr, John Dickson and Adrian Conan Doyle: *The Exploits of Sherlock Holmes.* New York: Random House, 1954. Perhaps the best attempts at pastiche ever written, mostly based on those fascinating mentions of unchronicled cases in the Canon and written by an ex pert mystery writer and Conan Doyle's son.

Dakin, D. Martin: *A Sherlock Holmes Commentary.* New York: Drake Publishers Inc., 1972. A fascinating and valuable reference book containing a technical commentary on each of the Holmes stories and novels with an attempt to date each.

DeWaal, Ronald: *The World Bibliography of Sherlock Holmes and Watson.* Boston: New York Graphic Society, 1974. An enormous and exhaustive work detailing books, recordings, plays, even films dealing with Holmes and Watson.

Hardwick, Michael and Mollie: *The Sherlock Holmes Companion.* London: John Murray, 1962. An in valuable reference book with story summaries, sampler of quotations, biographies of Holmes and Watson, and many of the original illustrations.

Harrison, Michael: *In the Footsteps of Sherlock Holmes*. New York: Frederick Fell, Inc., 1960. An excellent historical background on Holmes and entertaining travelogue based on Holmes' journeys; also valuable as enjoyable historical pieces are the author's other books, *The London of Sherlock Holmes* and *The World of Sherlock Holmes*.

Holroyd, James Edward: *Baker Street Byways*. London: George Allen & Unwin Ltd., 1959. An entertaining view of the London of Holmes' day.

Klinefelter, Walter: *Sherlock Holmes in Portrait and Profile*. New York: Syracuse University Press, 1963. An entertaining overview of the various illustrators and actors who have portrayed Holmes.

Starrett, Vincent: *The Private Life of Sherlock Holmes*. New York: The Macmillan Company, 1933. An excellent view of Holmes' life, times, and associates by one of the great Sherlockians.

PERIODICALS

The Baker Street Journal: New Series. Founded by Edgar W. Smith; presently edited by Julian Wolff, M.D. 33 Riverside Drive, New York, N.Y. 10023; official publication of the Baker Street Irregulars.

The Sherlock Holmes Journal. Edited by the Marquis of Donegall; The Studio, 3 Clabon Mews, London SW1. Official publication of the Sherlock Holmes Society of London.

www.ingramcontent.com/pod-product-compliance
Lightning Source LLC
LaVergne TN
LVHW011710060526
838200LV00051B/2834